Praise for **Leading Teams**

"Enjoyable to read. Simple to understand. Practical to implement. A must read for team members or leaders."

Debbie Fogel-Monnissen, Executive Vice President, International Markets Finance Officer, MasterCard, New York, USA

"A goldmine of practical business advice...clearly written, easy to read. Benefit from these winning strategies and proven solutions."

Barbara Large MBE, Senior Lecturer, Creative Writing; Honorary Fellow, University of Winchester; Chairman, Hampshire Writers' Society; Member, Royal Society of Arts, National Association of Writers in Education and The Society of Authors

"Leadership is about effective conversations. This book is a very useful ready reckoner for leaders everywhere seeking the words and methods needed each day at work."

Sanjay Gupta, CEO, English Helper Inc, Haryana, India

"This book described situations that are very familiar to me BUT.... gave me the tools to deal with them and the understanding of why they'd happened."

Dr Jane Neal-Smith, Head, School of Management, Guildhall Faculty of Business and Law, London Metropolitan University, London, UK

"Mandy and Elisabet are brilliant teachers and facilitators who have helped me build successful teams. Read this book to learn their powerful team building formula for success."

John W. Turner, Senior Vice President, Sales, TriNet, San Francisco, USA

"Real edgy scenarios that get to the heart of optimal team behaviours. In depth exploration and solutions from true experts."

Jackie Arnold, author, *Coaching Skills for Leaders in the Workplace,* ICF Executive Coach and Dip Coach Supervisor, www.coach4 executives.com, Hove, UK

"From reading this book and past experience of working with Mandy you learn there is never enough time to focus on what is strategic and important, unless you embed leading teams into how you work. Leaders reading this book will gain valuable insights into the small things that make a difference when leading teams to success."

Neal Watkins, Chief Product Officer and Executive Board Director, BAE Systems Applied Intelligence, UK

"This book is really, and literally, something else. Not the usual management fad. Instead, here is a manual with troubleshooting instructions within. I love that suggested solutions are taken down to what behaviours to display to make the solution come to life. The exemplifications of problems are spot on, and you can immediately recognise and relate to them. My team and I have worked a lot with creating team accountability and efficiency, and with the help of this manual we can continue to work with it on our own. My team members will get a copy as soon as the book is out."

Håkan Nyberg, Chief Executive Officer, Nordnet Bank, Stockholm, Sweden

"If you are looking for a 'how to' guide to improve your team's performance then this is the book for you. While many leadership and team building books are theoretical, *Leading Teams* provides sound principles and is filled with helpful hints and practical steps to enhance team dynamics and improve effectiveness. The advice and solutions in this book will work as effectively with a small team as with a large, globally distributed team."

Kristen Holden, business executive with 27 years in financial services, including insurance and banking, New York, USA

"I bought in from the first paragraph; ten chapters of real and practical examples on how to lead a team with characters skilfully portraying the tensions faced by leaders every day. A leadership masterclass."

Lynn Hill, Deputy CEO, West Hertfordshire Hospitals NHS Trust, Hertfordshire, UK

"Finally, a proactive approach to team leadership. The genius is that some solutions may seem almost too simple. Very engaging and useful."

Christina Skytt, CEO, international bestselling author, Executive Team Coach, Power Goals Academy, Stockholm, Sweden

"If you want to be great at leading people, then you have to read this book. Simple, powerful ideas to help you get the best out of your teams!"

Vinay Parmar, motivational business speaker and consultant, Get Vinspired!, Solihull, UK

Leading Teams

PEARSON

At Pearson, we believe in learning – all kinds of learning for all kinds of people. Whether it's at home, in the classroom or in the workplace, learning is the key to improving our life chances.

That's why we're working with leading authors to bring you the latest thinking and best practices, so you can get better at the things that are important to you. You can learn on the page or on the move, and with content that's always crafted to help you understand quickly and apply what you've learned.

If you want to upgrade your personal skills or accelerate your career, become a more effective leader or more powerful communicator, discover new opportunities or simply find more inspiration, we can help you make progress in your work and life.

Pearson is the world's leading learning company. Our portfolio includes the Financial Times and our education business, Pearson International.

Every day our work helps learning flourish, and wherever learning flourishes, so do people.

To learn more, please visit us at **www.pearson.com/uk**

The Financial Times

With a worldwide network of highly respected journalists, *The Financial Times* provides global business news, insightful opinion and expert analysis of business, finance and politics. With over 500 journalists reporting from 50 countries worldwide, our in-depth coverage of international news is objectively reported and analysed from an independent, global perspective.

To find out more, visit **www.ft.com/pearsonoffer/**

Leading Teams

10 Challenges: 10 Solutions

Mandy Flint and Elisabet Vinberg Hearn

PEARSON

Harlow, England • London • New York • Boston • San Francisco • Toronto • Sydney
Auckland • Singapore • Hong Kong • Tokyo • Seoul • Taipei • New Delhi
Cape Town • São Paulo • Mexico City • Madrid • Amsterdam • Munich • Paris • Milan

PEARSON EDUCATION LIMITED

Edinburgh Gate
Harlow CM20 2JE
United Kingdom
Tel: +44 (0)1279 623623
Web: www.pearson.com/uk

First edition published 2015 (print and electronic)
© Mandy Flint and Elisabet Vinberg Hearn 2015 (print and electronic)

ISBN: 978-1-292-08308-7 (print)
          978-1-292-08310-0 (PDF)
          978-1-292-08309-4 (eText)
          978-1-292-08311-7 (ePub)

British Library Cataloguing-in-Publication Data
A catalogue record for the print edition is available from the British Library

Library of Congress Cataloging-in-Publication Data
Flint, Mandy.
   Leading Teams: 10 challenges, 10 solutions / Mandy Flint and Elisabet Vinberg Hearn.
      pages cm
   Includes bibliographical references.
   ISBN 978-1-292-08308-7
   1. Teams in the workplace--Management. 2. Leadership. I. Hearn, Elisabet Vinberg. II. Title.
   HD66.F62 2015
   658.4'022--dc23
                                    2015022440
10 9 8 7 6 5 4 3 2 1
19 18 17 16 15

Cover design: Dan Mogford

Print edition typeset in 9/13 and Stone Serif ITC Pro Medium by 76
Print edition printed by Ashford Colour Press Ltd, Gosport

NOTE THAT ANY PAGE CROSS REFERENCES REFER TO THE PRINT EDITION

Contents

About the authors

Mandy Flint Mandy is an international expert on leading and developing teams. She is the CEO of Excellence in Leadership, a global transformational change organisation which she founded in 2000 after over 20 years of leadership experience in the corporate world. During this time Mandy spent 14 years working for American Express running business units and held roles in sales operations, public affairs, communications and cultural change.

As well as leading a business division within American Express as a senior leader, Mandy spent three years leading a cultural change transformation programme for the President as well as operating as an internal coach and team coach to many senior executive teams.

Through Excellence in Leadership Mandy works across the globe with both teams and individuals in the areas of one-to-one executive coaching, group training, team effectiveness, vision creation, strategic development and cultural change management. Her clients include CEOs, SVPs VPs and Board members in many multi-national blue-chip organisations, including MasterCard, Lloyds, American Express, Symantec, Virgin Atlantic, Hewlett Packard, SAP, G4, the NHS and Reuters.

Mandy studied at Harvard Business School focusing on the concept of the Service Profit Chain and has certification in the Tavistock Programme specialising in Advanced Process Consultancy. She is also media-trained and is an established speaker at leadership and cultural change events. She's a fellow at the London Metropolitan Business School and an award-winning author.

Elisabet Vinberg Hearn   Elisabet has extensive experience from the business world, including 13 years with American Express, based both in Sweden and in the UK. She has held various leadership roles, responsible for customer servicing, process re-engineering and corporate culture transformation.

She's founder of Think Solutions UK Ltd in the UK and Think Solutions AB in Sweden, leadership consultancies specialising in employee engagement and sustainable corporate cultures and leadership. She also operates as a consultant, speaker and coach, working with individuals, teams and organisations, providing strategic leadership and tactical solutions to clients around the World. Her consulting experience includes Executive Coaching, Leadership Team Dynamics and Effectiveness, Customer Service, Cultural Change, Cultural Intelligence, Visioning and Strategic Development. Her personal and professional style combined with considerable leadership experience has delivered lasting results for clients including; ABN AMRO, Royal Bank of Scotland, American Express, MasterCard, H&M, IKEA, Skanska, Vattenfall, Trygg-Hansa (Royal Sun Alliance) and Bombardier Transportation amongst others.

She has a degree in Marketing Economics from IHM Business School and an MBA in Leadership and Sustainability from the University of Cumbria (Robert Kennedy College) and is an award-winning author.

Introduction

Congratulations on deciding to read this book! You have taken a proactive approach to team leadership.

You see, you have two choices as a leader.

You can take a proactive or a reactive approach. The reactive way is the hopeful, passive way – hoping that the team will function well without any particular help or intervention from you. This approach rarely works, which is why we firmly recommend the proactive way, where you take charge and decide to create the climate and circumstances needed for your team to function successfully. And that's what this book is all about – successful teams. It gives you straight-talking solutions to those common team challenges, which you will be able to relate to.

We have worked with over 200 teams all over the world for the last 20 years, as well as leading teams ourselves for 25 years. In this book we have put together the ten challenges we most often see in teams that, unless addressed, will hinder the team from achieving consistent success. And as we have written this book together, we've been able to keep practicing teamwork ourselves too. We've continuously challenged each other and we have found that our ideas have triggered new ideas, and together we have created something much richer than we could have done individually.

Everyone is busy, we get that. The 'busy bug' is a common workplace disease, and becomes the excuse for not properly solving issues and challenges. Being busy is not the answer to great results though. So please, do yourself a favour; stop being busy and talking about being busy. By investing in your team up front, it makes you more effective and you can do less and achieve more.

The aim of this book is to help you address specific challenges you and your team may face. You can use it as a 'go to' source when you encounter a problem, and read the relevant chapter addressing the specific problem you have. Or you can, of course, choose to read the whole book if you are interested in getting your team to work as effectively as possible on all fronts.

Each chapter explores the problem, thoughts and feelings of team members, and gives solutions and behavioural suggestions. There's also self-assessment and reflection questions to help you think through the challenge more specifically as it pertains to your team. This is how each chapter is structured:

- Chapter outcomes
- Self-assessment
- Example of problem
- Exploring the problem
- Solutions
- Behaviours of team and leader
- Thoughts and feelings of team and leader
- Summary
- Reflection questions
- Self-assessment

Some solutions may seem almost 'too simple' and straightforward, but don't be fooled; sometimes it is the simple solutions that get overlooked as we often think 'it must be more complicated than that'. We recommend that you look at these simple but effective, proven solutions and implement them. If you do, they can have a major impact on your team.

As you start reading the book, you will find that certain challenges and their solutions link to other challenges and solutions. This is natural. Team dynamics are fluid and as a result, when you start working on one aspect of your team effectiveness, it can have a positive knock-on effect on another area. On the flip side, this also means that even if you only face one of these challenges, unless you address it, it may create other challenges.

Team dynamics are fluid and therefore require continuous work. The most successful teams are constantly reviewing how they are doing, and making necessary adjustments.

What has got us to where we are today as a team, is not going to take us to where we need to be tomorrow and into the future.

If you want to achieve real, lasting change, pay particular attention to behaviours. How we behave and conduct ourselves have an impact on others, creating a ripple effect. It's when we change our daily behaviours that we can achieve transformational change.

This book applies to all levels in an organisation. It doesn't matter if you are the CEO, a middle manager, new to leadership or a team member – this book has something practical to offer for everyone.

Above all, when reading this book, don't just read it!

It's only when you implement the solutions that the book will show its true value.

Reading about it, thinking about it will not do it – you have to do it.

Even a single person in a team, doing something different and powerful, can start to make a difference and influence team members to do the same. And remember, even doing something seemingly small and simple, can have a big impact.

When you start implementing these solutions, you are acquiring transferable team skills which you can take with you into future teams too.

We wish you great team success.

Acknowledgements

There are a number of people whom we want to acknowledge for helping us make this book a reality.

Thank you Karen Ancell for your invaluable help with feedback, editing and creative ideas for improvements.

Thanks to all our clients and colleagues who constantly inspire us and makes us want to go to work.

Thank you David Crosby and Nicole Eggleton of Pearson Education for asking us to write this book.

Thanks to our family and friends who have encouraged us to keep writing and supported us so that we can!

Thank you Mark Shelmerdine for sharing your expertise in publishing with us once again.

Thank you Barbara Large for your inspiration and support in both writing and publishing.

We would also like thank the Society of Authors for their help and guidance.

The photo in Figure 7.2 is by 123rf.com

How do you build trust?

- Building rapport and trust
- Encouraging openness and honesty
- Improving collaboration

'Either we're a team or we're not. Either you trust me or you don't.'

Ally Carter

Self-assessment

Before reading the chapter, do the following quick self-assessment.

How would you rate the following in your team?

	1 Very poor	2 Poor	3 Just OK	4 Good	5 Excellent
Openness					
Trust level					
Honesty					
Respect					
Interaction					

A team on paper only

The meeting hadn't started yet, and the 14 people around the table were all on their smartphones or laptops. They were tapping away or had their phone headsets on, acting as a barrier to shield themselves from their immediate surroundings. Apart from two people having a hushed conversation, there was no other interaction going on between the people around the table.

The group was waiting for their leader Davide to turn up. He had summoned them here for a monthly team meeting. All working for a French construction company, they were based in different locations around Europe. They had officially been a team for three months and had met on several occasions and yet, with the exception of a couple of people, they didn't know each other at all. Their average age was late 40s and there was a wealth of industry experience in the room. It represented a gold mine of opportunities for this team to be very successful.

▶ There was a sudden burst of energy as the door flew open. Heads turned towards Davide, their leader, as he raced into the room, pulling out his earphones while finishing a conversation in an abrupt manner: 'I need to go now. I'm starting a meeting, talk later.'

His dramatic entrance was met by raised heads followed by a quick return to what they had been doing before.

'OK, let's get started. We have a lot to get through and not much time.' He rattled through the agenda, which was far too ambitious, making everyone painfully aware that they weren't going to be able to do all of it. Everyone nodded as none of them was courageous enough to say what they really thought.

There was no chitchat going on, which meant Davide could get started straight away on his list of agenda topics. And he didn't invite any small talk either. Going around the room, each person was asked to give an individual update. This was mostly in the form of a dialogue with Davide, and no one else intervened. The other 13 people were like an unwilling audience, some of them still on their smartphones which they now held under the table.

Why do I have to be here? This is a waste of my time. I have so much to do. I wonder what my team is doing now, I should have been there instead. I can't wait until this weekend and some time off. Is it really three hours to lunch? Oh, here we go again, another boring update!

These were some of the thoughts running through the minds of those present.

Davide continued to move the agenda along, listening to each person's update, asking some questions and then moving on, never encouraging any interaction or sharing, simply expecting a straight-forward report. Fred was half way through his update, when he mentioned how some key metrics of the production scorecard were improving at the manufacturing plant in Germany.

Jon was suddenly paying attention. The information had filtered through to him despite his apathy, and the reason was he knew straight away that Fred was not telling the truth. Jon had been at the plant the previous week and knew these metrics had not improved. He had even participated in a meeting where this had been discussed. Jon felt ▶

> ▶   acutely uncomfortable but tried to hide his reaction. He didn't know Fred, he didn't even know Davide very well or any of the others; and he didn't feel he could bring this up. He asked himself why Fred would not be sharing the true state of affairs with this team. *He must have his reasons,* he thought. But as he didn't know or trust him, he decided to keep quiet, making a mental note to tread carefully in this team.

Exploring the problem

In the example above, the group of people is a team on paper, but not really functioning like a team in reality. The lack of interaction suggests they are a group of strangers rather than an effective team.

There are some obvious issues with how this team is acting and behaving. These issues apply to many teams.

Interaction

There is no natural chitchat. Even though they are all in the room together, only two people are talking to each other.

There is no eye contact between people. They are even actively avoiding it by getting stuck into their gadgets instead. And without eye contact, no real contact can be made.

They are all doing their own thing, reading emails, talking on the phone – the way people do when they sit on a train with strangers.

Respect

When the updates are being made, they are not interested in or respectful of each other and each other's updates. They are not paying attention and they are instead on their smartphones under the table. You could argue that if everyone is doing the same thing, no harm is done, but the fact is that most people would still find it disrespectful if it was done to them.

The team snubs their leader as he enters the room, but he doesn't really notice that. He is not attuned to or aware of what is going on in the room.

Leader behaviours

The leader is late, but doesn't apologise or comment on this. He seems unaware of the fact that it could annoy people that he has left them waiting. And as he has not spent any time bonding with the team, they will be less forgiving of this kind of behaviour.

Davide's agenda is his own rather than that of the whole team. He's not involving the others in the agenda or asking for any input. This makes the team members feel like order takers rather than mature contributors.

Any interaction is purely one-to-one rather than inclusive of the team. The conversation flows between leader and individual team members only.

Openness

The limited interaction between team members means there is limited exchange of experience and the team is not benefiting from the extensive experience represented in the room.

Information is not honestly shared, as represented in the last two paragraphs of the example. And when people realise that, they get cautious and suspicious.

Dishonest disclosures are not challenged. Even though Jon knows that Fred is not telling the truth, he keeps quiet, which further stops any effective teamwork.

These actions and behaviours do not lead to trust and if they continue over time they create active distrust, which is counter-productive to effective teams and team results.

Teams where people don't trust each other don't create teamwork, they just create work. And more work than needed. Pretty silly, huh?

The reasons for lack of trust in teams

The first common reason for lack of trust is simply that people don't know each other. It's hard to trust someone you don't know. In this example, the members of the team are simply individuals reporting to the same person, nothing more nothing less. They don't know each other and are showing no wish to change that.

There are of course a number of problems with such a scenario. If people don't know each other, then they don't understand each other, and they don't want to engage or take an interest, because they haven't made that human connection. Therefore they don't trust each other.

A human connection happens when two or more people meet and talk to each other about more than just the facts. In the example above, Davide is simply asking for a factual update. This process means that they are not *relating* to those facts, they are only *relaying* them. It's transactional rather than relationship driven. Mere facts may interest people but will rarely engage them on an emotional level. As a result they are unlikely to share information with each other unless they have to, good or bad. This leads to a hesitance to share what they know, which creates a lack of trust. This means they never get to know each other outside the factual dialogue and can't create an effective relationship, let alone a working one. Would *you* choose to work in those circumstances?

A brilliant working relationship demands a great personal relationship, as people don't leave their persona at home when they come to work. Additionally, when people bring their thoughts and feelings to the team, it provides more valuable information about the subject and it becomes easier for people to relate to. This makes them more engaged and willing to participate, sharing their knowledge and experience. It's a win–win strategy that benefits the individual, the team and ultimately the business and its customers.

The reasons why team members don't know each other

Here are the top reasons:

- They just want to get on with the job tasks, and are not seeing working relationships as part of that job.
- They are busy enough as it is when they meet.
- It's not encouraged by leaders or others.
- They don't see it as important, they don't see the point.

- They don't prioritise it.
- Personality differences exist.
- Negative first impressions have been formed and can be hard to change.
- Egos get in the way of connecting with others.

Whatever the reason, not knowing each other has an impact.

The impact of team members not knowing each other

- They withhold information and also don't share their ideas and experiences with each other.
- They don't feel comfortable telling the truth. This doesn't necessarily mean that they are lying or having a negative intent. It simply means they are cautious with what they say for fear of the reaction they will get. This could be the result of previous experience where truth was not welcome, where a leader 'shot the messenger', didn't like what he/she heard and punished the person who was being honest. It could also be because they are noticing that others are not telling the truth.
- They miss out on opportunities for quick answers and resolutions to problems. In the example above, Jon actually has previous experience and connections, which could help resolve the issues at the German plant quickly and easily. As Fred doesn't know this he doesn't invite Jon's input. And, as Jon doesn't know how Fred will react, he doesn't offer.
- What is interesting to remember is that the behaviours described here are not always conscious, intentional behaviours; they are often merely part of a survival or coping strategy. We will look further into behaviours later on in this chapter and throughout the book.

The impact on the business, its customers, employees and stakeholders

When people don't know or trust each other it leads to a hesitance or unwillingness to work together, which makes it hard to perform even the simplest of tasks.

In a recent situation that we observed, a team member expressed frustration as she felt her team members were dismissive about the importance of her work. This disinterest was a result of the team members not knowing each other, rather than them being intentionally dismissive. Not realising this, she felt angry, defensive and helpless, which made things even worse. Subsequently she didn't want to work with them and started to avoid them, which impacted communication and team spirit even further.

Ultimately this affected one of their clients, who didn't get a promised report on time, because communication had broken down between the colleagues. The client complained about the breach of contract this entailed and a penalty clause kicked in which meant the client didn't have to pay.

That's the link between the lack of trust and the bottom line. It's not the only one though.

The lack of cooperation means it takes longer to get the work done, which affects productivity, which in turn affects costs.

And let's not forget that when trust is low, loyalty is low too, leading to higher employee turnover, which leads to more costs. There are the costs of hiring and training new people. There are also costs related to loss of knowledge and experience that impact the customers and their loyalty and spend. This link between lack of trust and additional cost is rarely made by leaders.

Let's look at another example, involving a team member who we will call Howard. Howard felt so alienated from his silo-working team, there was no sense of belonging, which made him think: *Why should I do things for them, when they are not doing anything for me?* This made Howard feel as if he was in it alone. He had no attachment to the team and therefore no obvious desire to stay. He jumped ship as soon as another job offer came up. He walked away with crucial knowledge that was no longer available to that team, and it took them a year to close the knowledge gap. It was a very costly process, all a result of lack of trust and loyalty across the team.

In really extreme cases, lack of trust will also lead to the loss of customers. Enough said.

Solutions

A team needs to spend time together, and it is important to invest time in getting to know each other in order to trust each other. It's actually that simple. If you are the leader of a team, you can make this happen by recognising that it needs some thought and follow-through. It is simple to do.

Let's get specific on how to do it.

Solution 1: Encourage your team members to talk

Whether you are a leader or a member of the team, you can be the one that takes that initiative in encouraging team members to talk. It isn't rocket science, it is as easy as that. It just takes someone to start it, someone needs to step up to the plate and be the hero, the one that makes it happen.

This can happen in team meetings, where it can form a regular spot on the agenda. It can also be encouraged through having employees buddy up on job tasks where talking can happen naturally as part of working together. And one of the most effective ways to get people to talk is to show genuine interest in them by asking questions. Tread carefully though – asking too many questions can sound like an interrogation, no matter how well intended they are. Pick one or two to get the conversation going, and take it from there.

Some questions that work:

- So, what did you do before you started working here?
- Where do you come from?
- Where did you go to school?
- What was your very first job?
- Did you always intend to work in (this industry)?
- What do you do outside of work, do you have any particular hobbies/interests?
- Where do you live?

- What do you think we could be doing differently as a team?
- What do you enjoy the most with your job?
- If you could do anything, what would you do?
- If you were CEO, what would you change about how we do business?

Solution 2: Disclosure breeds disclosure, leading to greater openness

If you want others to talk and share, you need to first share something about yourself and not just your work image, but something about you as a person. You need to demonstrate trust to get trust; if you trust them with personal information about you, they are more likely to do the same. As mentioned earlier, you can do this in meetings, over lunch, during informal huddles, in the lift or while waiting for the bus. People are naturally curious about each other and if you show that it's OK to talk about yourself, people will feel good that you were interested enough in them to share something about you.

Solution 3: If openness is lacking where you work, you can decide what you are willing and prepared to share

Work cultures can vary greatly and some cultures are naturally open and trustful. In such a culture, opening up is easier and forms part of the norm. In more guarded cultures though, where people have learnt to watch their words, it would be unwise to be too open as this may be met by surprise or even suspicion and could be damaging for the person's standing in the organisation. A safe starting point is sharing work knowledge and experience; you can progress through to more personal disclosure as trust grows. You can also praise people for opening up when they do it, as this can encourage others to do the same.

Solution 4: Decide to invest in building relationships

Taking time to get to know people is critical and yet people often see it as a waste of time. If you change your way of thinking and instead think of relationship building as part of the job, then you're not in danger of seeing it as a time-consuming addition to the job and avoid it. It is simply a part of being successful, by creating a great team environment where work can be more effectively performed. Think about when an issue arises at work; it often comes down to resolving the issue by going to the person you know, whom you have the best relationship with and who you trust will be able to help you. This then allows you to resolve the issue quickly and more efficiently. So make the investment, carve out time for building relationships unless it's already part of your daily agenda.

Solution 5: You must spend time on getting to know each other

Do this outside of formal agendas and business meetings. You need to create informal opportunities to spend time together as well. These can include:

- Office breakfasts
- Lunches
- Huddles
- Coffee/tea breaks together
- Drinks after work
- Dinner
- Sports
- Other social activities.

Keep in mind that for many people it's hard to meet up outside of work hours and this *is* part of work after all. It doesn't have to be very time consuming, but it needs to be regular. Some teams even have a rule that says 'we are not to talk about work' during these social informal times together. Realistically this can be tough sometimes, so some teams put money into a hat every time someone talks about work, then they donate that money to charity.

Solution 6: Explain why it's so important to know each other in order to work well together

You need to carve out the time needed and you need to be explicit about what you're doing, so that the team knows why it's important to know each other. Create an interest in it, help people to feel how beneficial it is, share examples of where it's been useful and successful

– invite the team members to share their examples. People can often remember a time when they were in a powerful team and remember how well they knew each other and what that created for them. Team members don't always make the links from knowing each other to being part of a successful team, so help them see that link.

Solution 7: Keep promises

There's nothing quite as powerful when it comes to building trust, as doing what you promised. When promises are met, other people can relax, safe in the conviction that they know what is expected and what they can expect. So holding each other to account and doing what you say you will do is part of knowing each other. If I know I can rely on you, then I understand you better and know you better, and therefore I have greater trust. So creating an environment where promises are made and kept is important. Even using the word promise rather than commitment makes a difference. There is something very powerful in saying 'I promise'.

Solution 8: Stop sticking your head in the sand (if you are)

Having team members who know and trust each other is not just a 'nice to have', it is a crucial business strategy. It's your job. You could leave it to luck, but let's be frank, success is rarely, if ever, down to luck. Actively consider the benefits you can reap by getting proper 'teaming' to happen in your team. The team members don't need to be best friends, they just need to know and on some level like each other.

Let's look at the team we met earlier and see how they employed this solution.

A month after the meeting in Champagne, Davide had organised another team meeting. On the agenda this time was simply 'getting to know each other'. That was it. Everyone had received the invite and no one was sure what to expect with the apparent lack of regular business issues on the agenda.

There was an initial hesitation when people walked into the room, as the layout was very different from previous meetings. Where meeting rooms normally have a table in the middle, this room had 14 chairs arranged in the shape of a horseshoe, and no table in sight. There was nowhere to hide.

This time the team didn't have to wait for Davide, he was already in the room with plenty of time to spare. He welcomed them and asked them to take a seat.

Gingerly they started to take their positions in the horseshoe. There was some jostling of chairs as a few people readjusted theirs. Some even moved their chairs slightly outside the circle, as if to already distance themselves from this unfamiliar process.

Jon awkwardly tried to find somewhere to put his notepad, and ended up putting it under his chair.

Fred felt exposed and realised that he wouldn't be able to sneak onto his smartphone without everyone noticing.

Davide explained that this team meeting was different from the previous ones, that they needed to get to know and trust each other in order to be a well-functioning team.

He then continued by asking his team members to talk in pairs, and to reveal something about their professional as well as their personal life that the others wouldn't know. Afterwards they would be sharing the information with the whole team.

Later, Davide led the way by sharing that his first job had been working as a ski guide in Courchevel. There were some surprised smiles, followed by some mumbled comments of 'I had no idea!', coupled with the more direct comment of 'I didn't have you down as a ski bum, Davide!', which was rewarded with his chuckle. This demonstrated to everyone that it was OK to be open with each other. Davide then continued to deepen his story by elaborating on how he met Francesca, his wife, on the slopes, and how they still enjoy skiing whenever they can. 'Next year we are going to Canada for the first time,' he said.

'What, the whole team?' said Fred and winked. He was beginning to enjoy the more relaxed atmosphere.

Davide grinned, 'I'm not sure what Francesca would say!' He surveyed the room, noticing that everyone was paying attention, there was not a single smartphone in sight. *It's working,* he thought.

▶ Over the next 30 minutes it was revealed that Fred was an avid guitar player who used to be in a band, that Tom loved sailing and had a big boat, that Alain had been a junior French tennis champion, along with many other interesting stories. Surprisingly, they found they had more in common than they would have previously thought.

After some laughter and friendly teasing, the atmosphere had changed. It had become easier to talk and they moved their conversation into the plans for the next year. Greater interest was shown than in previous meetings. Everyone had input and Davide noticed that there was more direct conversation between people than he had observed before. It was a good start. He knew there was more work to be done, but he was pleasantly surprised by how effective this simple approach had been. It was definitely a good start.

Behaviours of team and leader

Under 'Solutions' above, we have listed a number of 'how to' actions. These solutions work best when carried out with these supporting 'how to' behaviours. The solutions on their own will only get you so far. With the right behaviours you will speed up the process of building familiarity and trust.

'How to' solutions	'How to' behaviours	How the behaviours make the difference
Encourage your team members to talk.	Listening Showing interest	When showing genuine interest and listening actively, you make the other person feel important – and they will realise that their input matters, that it's a good thing for them to talk.
Disclosure breeds disclosure, leading to greater openness.	Showing courage	If you have the courage to share more than surface-level information, maybe even talking about something that shows you as being not perfect, others can do the same and you can start having more real conversations that don't skirt over the issues.

▶

'How to' solutions	'How to' behaviours	How the behaviours make the difference
If openness is lacking where you work, you can decide what you are willing and prepared to share.	Showing courage Showing social awareness	As in the previous example, this takes some level of courage. Being socially aware is about understanding the undertones of your organisation, so that you don't expose yourself too much too soon and therefore damage your credibility. It means that you can read the implicit rules and tread carefully for best, gradual results.
You must spend time on getting to know each other.	Showing empathy	Spending time together in itself means you get to know each other better. This time spent, while showing empathy, changes the dynamics in relationships and opens up dialogue, dialogue that otherwise may not happen.
Explain why it's so important to know each other in order to work well together.	Using openness and transparency	If you are open about why you are taking time out to get the team together, you are appealing to the human need for 'reason'. It is human nature to want to know why.
Keep promises.	Demonstrating trust	Promise is an emotional word and hits you at an emotional level. There is nothing as powerful as a promise kept, being trustworthy. And a promise broken breaks trust. Either way it affects trust at the core level.
Stop sticking your head in the sand! (if you are).	Showing courage	A trustful team is not a 'nice to have', it is a crucial part of the job. It is your job. Show courage by making sure any trust issues get addressed.

We've focused here on useful behaviours when it comes to creating familiarity and trust.

When intentionally practised over time, they become powerful, impactful habits that happen naturally.

Thoughts and feelings of team and leader

On average, a person experiences around 70,000 thoughts per day.[1]

Many of those thoughts are habits that affect a person's mindset or outlook.

What we think affects how we feel, and how we feel affects how we think.

When wanting to improve familiarity and trust within a team, actively replace thoughts and feelings that are counterproductive to that. Here are thoughts from the story, their impact on feelings and how they can be changed.

Negative thoughts	Negative feelings	Powerful thoughts	Powerful feelings
Why do I have to be here?	Frustration, helplessness	*How can I make the most of being here?*	Hope, curiosity
This is a waste of my time. I have so much to do.	Stress, anger	*I participate 100 per cent wherever I am, as I don't like to waste my time. OR I stay in this moment, focusing on now. I'll get to the other things later.*	Calm, content
This is so painful to listen to.	Pain, frustration	*I am taking an interest in this. OR I am going to find the 'diamond' in this.*	Curiosity, surprise
Our new leader is just too young! What does he know anyway?	Worry, jealousy	*What new things could I learn from him, making the most of his youth and new outlook?*	Hope, trust, surprise
Fred is lying about the scorecard!	Disgust, anxiety	*I will talk to Fred to clarify this situation.*	Content, hope
If he's not telling, I'm not telling.	Fear, anxiety	*I could start by giving a little away.*	Excitement

Summary

Team awareness

Team members absolutely need to know each other, both professionally and personally.

If people don't know each other, then they don't understand each other, and they don't want to engage or take an interest, because they haven't made that human connection. As a result they don't trust each other.

Team building

A team needs to spend time getting to know each other. This can happen in team meetings, in-house or offsite, through formal and informal get-togethers. Teams we've worked with have monthly dinners, weekly breakfasts etc. They ensure that they have lunch with each other regularly, as a whole team as well as one-to-one. Sometimes they even ban talking about work, and keep it at a purely personal level – those are the teams that enjoy each other's company the most and perform the best.

According to Gallup's study on Employee Engagement [2], one of the 12 employee engagement factors is, 'I have a best friend at work'.

It does have an impact on the bottom line

In our example, there is a direct correlation between people knowing each other and trust and the bottom line. We can make many links every day from a behaviour, and follow that link through to the effect on the bottom line. All of our solutions and actions in this chapter demonstrate how important it is for people to build trust. So don't leave it to chance. You wouldn't leave an important business meeting to chance, would you?

Reflection questions for the reader

Look at your team and consider:

- How well do people know and trust each other generally?
- How well do they/we know each other personally (beyond work roles)?
- What can I do to create more openness and trust?
- What behaviours am I demonstrating to create more trust?

- What can I do to let others get to know me?
- What role am I playing in the team's current level of openness and trust?
- How much time am I devoting to getting to know my team/ colleagues?

Self-assessment

After you have implemented the solutions in this chapter, answer these questions again to see the progress you have made.

How would you rate the following in your team?

	1 Very poor	2 Poor	3 Just OK	4 Good	5 Excellent
Openness					
Trust level					
Honesty					
Respect					
Interaction					

How do you overcome conflicts or tensions?

- Improving communication
- Encouraging open-mindedness
- Understanding others' perspectives
- Increasing healthy debate that leads to better results

'Everything has beauty, but not everyone sees it.'

Confucius

Self-assessment

Before reading the chapter, do the following quick self-assessment.

How would you rate the following in your team?

	1 Very poor	2 Poor	3 Just OK	4 Good	5 Excellent
Communication					
Healthy debating					
Constructive disagreement					
Open-mindedness					

Threatened by the arrival of a new colleague

I don't feel comfortable around the new guy. I don't know what to make of him. Why has Harriet brought her old colleague into this team? What is she playing at? Surely we already had all the capable people we needed? Or is she saying that we are not capable enough? Is she trying to change the team? What does this mean for me? I think I need to talk this over with Clark.

Sarah sent an instant message to Clark and was pleased to find out that he was indeed available for a quick call.

Her phone shook as Clark's name appeared on its screen.

'Hi Clark!' she said in a hushed tone. She looked around the office to see who was around and might overhear the call. Thankfully only a few people were present, seated the other end of the office space. She hunched over her desk, pushing her phone close to her ear.

After some initial pleasantries, she got to the subject she wanted to discuss.

▶ 'What do you think of Rob and how he was brought in?'

'Why are you asking? Has he ruffled your feathers?' Clark responded with a smile in his voice.

Sarah was very quick to retort: 'No, no, no, not at all. But were you aware of how well they got on when they worked together before? You know that Harriet was a peer of Rob's, don't you?'

'Yes, I know that. And I don't think that needs to be a problem.' Clark sounded calm.

'Well, I think it might already be a problem, as I have heard that Rob will be given the EXODUS project.' She paused for effect and continued. 'This is something Harriet should have kept for herself as it needs handling at her level. Or if she was going to hand it over to anyone, it should have gone to me, or maybe you. We have more experience in this company than he does, and that is what matters in this case after all.'

'Maybe, maybe not. It could be that his external view will give it another dimension that we couldn't give it. He's got loads of experience, just not in our company. And I like him, he's seems like a nice guy.'

Sarah felt frustrated to not get Clark's agreement, but didn't say so. The frustration was further added to as Clark cut the conversation short to rush to a meeting.

I was expecting Clark to agree with me. How annoying that he didn't! I thought I could rely on him. Never mind, I'm going to show Harriet that I'm better than Rob. Besides, I'm sure he's not as perfect as Harriet is trying to make out that he is. I'm sure I can find something less than flattering under the surface. And I don't need Clark any way. I'm going to go find someone else in the team who will agree with me and see the truth.

Exploring the problem

In the example above, conflict and tension are brought into the team with the perceived threat of a new team member.

Conflict and tension can have many different causes and this can play itself out in many varied forms. Sometimes it can be an open, argumentative conflict and sometimes it can be in a passive aggressive form, where it's less obvious and therefore more difficult to address.

Most teams and team members will experience conflict and tension regularly.

Let's explore what is going on in this example.

Intrapersonal tension

Sarah feels threatened by the arrival of a new colleague. The threat is created by the fact that her boss knew this person from before. Sarah believes that they had a close working bond which means she and the other team members may not be as valued as him, as they don't have that close bond.

It is not clear to either Sarah or Clark why Rob has been brought in, which creates unnecessary speculation.

Rob and Harriet have previously been peers, which makes Sarah look at him as someone more senior than herself. This makes her compare herself to him and worry that she is not good enough. She feels inferior yet wants to make out as if she isn't by saying that she should have been given the EXODUS project.

Comparing herself to her new colleague moves Sarah into a competitive mindset, not one with a win–win focus.

Impact on time and productivity

Time is wasted as Sarah and Clark are removing themselves from their job to discuss this. Productivity is therefore affected.

Trust levels

When Clark suggests that Sarah feels threatened by Rob, she denies it. By not being transparent, she creates tension between them, as it's obvious to him that she is not truthful.

As Sarah doesn't know or trust Rob very well yet, she doesn't feel she can address him directly with any of her thoughts, which means her sense of conflict is greater than it needs to be.

Additionally, she doesn't approach her boss with any of her concerns, which means no real clarification can happen. She doesn't approach her boss for fear of how the boss will react. After all, Harriet, the boss, has brought in a person whom she has worked with before so there is an existing relationship at play. Also, the boss might not know that this much conflict is going on.

Because Sarah doesn't know Rob very well, she makes assumptions based on hearsay. She's putting pieces of information together that aren't necessarily true, and they create a fabricated picture that she starts to believe.

When taking the call from Clark, Sarah looks around the room to make sure no one can hear, which indicates that she knows that her conversation could provoke reactions in the team. This is an indication of a low level of openness.

Interpersonal tension

When Sarah can't get Clark to agree with her perceived assessment, she experiences further conflict and tension.

By not agreeing with Sarah, Clark is trying to get her to look at the situation more constructively, but as a result he is creating more conflict as he expresses a different opinion.

Sarah creates more tension by looking for someone to collude with. When she can't get Clark to agree, she decides to look for another ally.

Even a short, simple example such as this one, demonstrates how much conflict and tension can be created and multiplied in any situation.

So what does this mean for you and your team?

The reasons for conflict and tension in teams

Conflict is simply a difference of opinion. An opinion in and of itself is neither good nor bad. It's the interpretation that could create a negative sense of conflict.

Here are the top reasons for conflict and tension in teams:

Lack of communication

When they are not given enough information, people will fill in the gaps and make it up, even if they don't know that they are making it up. The mind is quick to piece together any bits of data, no matter how small, and make up its own story. Each person is different from the next, so we build our own story uniquely, if we haven't been given the whole picture. In the story, Harriet, the leader, had not explained well enough to her team why she had brought Rob in and what he brings to the team.

Another communication issue is when people do not communicate their thoughts and concerns, which could provide the clarification they need to avoid a sense of conflict. The example above showed how Sarah was guilty of this.

Virtual teams can experience conflict because of the lack of face-to-face and non-verbal communication. When people don't have access to non-verbal clues there is more risk of misunderstanding, which creates conflict.

Personal differences

As mentioned before, everyone is unique and it's important to understand how that creates differences in teams. If a person doesn't understand another team member and his/her personal needs and values, they look at his/her opinions and behaviours as flawed as they don't match the person's own view. Truly stepping into somebody else's shoes and seeing things from their angle is not an easy task. The pace and speed at which we operate, doesn't always allow us to be in the moment to be able to do that. So this is an understandable challenge we all face, but that's not an excuse for not doing it.

Conflicting goals

If team members have differing goals, i.e. goals that for some reason don't support each other, then their priorities will differ and they will not see the importance of the other person's task. This creates conflict or at least tension.

This is often the case in matrix organisations, where people work together across teams and business areas, thereby becoming part of several different teams. This is where conflicting goals are often a reality, as there is not enough alignment of goals and focus higher up in the organisation.

Competitive behaviours

When roles are unclear, people end up doing the same things as other team members because it's not clear who owns what and therefore who is supposed to do what. This in turn makes people feel like they are competing for the task and conflict is almost guaranteed, especially if communication is lacking.

Conflict arises from the idea that something is either right or wrong, which in turn means that when opinions differ *someone* is either right or wrong. And when people think like that, they want to be right. When they go for the need to be right, they no longer look for the potential value in someone else's view. Assuming both parties want to be right, tension is then created by *both* of them not feeling listened to or valued.

Competitive behaviour also happens when team members feel they have to prove themselves. As in the example above, this can be caused by a new person whose perceived seniority creates a sense of inferiority or self-doubt in someone else. Another example of this could be if a team member achieves better results than another. This would bring out competitive behaviours that are no longer about the good of the team. The focus is only on 'what's in it for me'.

The impact of conflict and tension in teams

If conflict and tension are not managed, they erode trust and make people work on their own rather than cooperate. In really bad cases it also makes people work against each other.

This is how a team is impacted by conflict and tension:

■ People waste time thinking about it and often also talking to others about it, and thus create more tension.

■ When people don't have enough information and they make up their own story, rumours are created and suspicion grows, which is detrimental to teamwork.

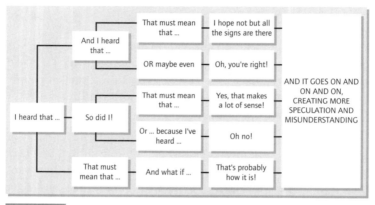

Figure 2.1 The misunderstanding multiplier

■ When people don't ask for information or fail to voice concerns, the issue festers and continues to drive team members apart.

■ If people don't understand each other, they don't interact and the team is therefore less efficient.

■ Conflicting goals create confusion, which leads to inactivity, which affects productivity.

■ Competitive behaviour where team members have a personal agenda that doesn't match the team's agenda is deeply divisive and has a negative effect on team spirit.

The impact on the business, customers, employees and stakeholders

When there is conflict in a team, others are bound to notice. Conflict or tension is rarely comfortable for others to watch, so the team could risk damaging important relationships.

Let's look at an example of how team conflict affects the customer's experience.

A group of friends were out to dinner at a well-known restaurant. Two waiters were serving at their table, which created some confusion. Although they had been given menus, they were not able to order their food for over 20 minutes. The friends overheard the waiters squabbling about who should take their orders. Eventually one of the waiters came to their table, reluctantly. The food arrived, accompanied by continued arguments between the two waiters, making the dinner party determined to just ignore them. In fact, they were even making fun of the situation as it was so obvious; it was like watching kids in a playground. Other diners started to point and laugh at the waiters. When asked if they wanted dessert, the group discussed their options and decided to go elsewhere as they didn't want to be part of the conflict anymore – they just wanted a nice evening out. The group organiser felt let down and embarrassed having chosen this really cool restaurant for dinner. They left and they ended up telling this story to a number of other people, so there were repercussions for the brand/image as well as a financial impact on the restaurant. When it came to the tip, the group laughed and no conversation was needed; no way would they be leaving a tip. The impact of no tip directly affected the revenue and the waiters' pockets too.

This simple but illuminating example demonstrates how overt conflict makes other people feel.

Within organisations, conflict can have an equally bad effect. Other teams may avoid working with tension-ridden teams where possible, as it's hard work. It takes too long to get people on side, to get things done, to come to agreements.

This is how it might work.

Andrew was an inspirational manager. His team loved him and he had high hopes for what the team would be able to achieve. Andrew more or less promised Kevin a promotion in the upcoming reorganisation.

> ▶ Kevin felt proud and motivated as a result and worked all hours to
> show Andrew that he had made the right decision. When it came to
> it, Andrew didn't deliver as he promised and gave the promotion to
> someone else. Kevin was furious, but didn't confront Andrew. Instead
> he let the anger bubble inside and he stopped working as hard. He
> also started avoiding Andrew whenever he could, almost drawing their
> communication to a complete stop. He didn't talk to anyone else about
> it, but it became obvious to his colleagues that something was going
> on and those who dared to ask were quickly assured that nothing was
> wrong. This made them even more concerned and the tension spread
> in the team. The marketing team, who had close collaboration with
> Andrew's team, started noticing that something was wrong. After a
> few frustrating meetings, where Kevin had been in a bad mood while
> his colleagues exchanged glances, one of the marketing managers
> decided to bypass Kevin and his colleagues next time around. As a
> result, the marketing team started doing some of the work for Andrew's
> team, which created unclear roles; these overlaps, along with further
> irritation, had an impact on productivity.

In this example, poor communication between Andrew and
Kevin leads to passive aggressive conflict, which may be
harder to address than open conflict. The knock-on effects
are many: work-around, role confusion, communication gaps.
All waste time and effort and have a negative impact on the
bottom line.

Solutions

Conflict and tension doesn't have to be a bad thing. It can
even be healthy, if carefully managed, as it can trigger healthy
debates and make people think differently. Knowledge and
insight can expand, innovation can happen and results
flourish. So the point is not to avoid conflict at all cost, it is to
manage it in such a way that it becomes a powerful vehicle for
teamwork.

Let's get specific on how to do it.

Solution 1: Communicate, communicate, communicate

In order to fill in the communication gaps that others will otherwise fill with their own assumptions, you need to communicate, communicate, communicate. Don't be afraid to state the obvious, because it may not be obvious to others. Don't make the assumption that people already know. People always want the context, the reason why something is happening, so put particular focus here.

Solution 2: Get together and ask constructive questions

Instead of assuming, ask questions. Frame questions constructively to get the information you need, to fill the communication gap.

And if you notice that a colleague is avoiding you or seems concerned, invest the time to get together talk to him/her. And if you are noticing that there are tensions in the team as a whole, get together and talk. Ask open questions that make people open up.

Here are some questions that work for both teams and individuals:

■ How are you doing?

■ What's going on for you right now?

■ Is there anything we need to talk about?

■ Is there anything I need to know about?

■ Is there anything you need from me right now?

■ What's working well for us right now?

■ What could be better? What's not working so well?

■ How can I help you?

■ How can we help each other?

Solution 3: Assume positive intent

Everyone is different. Just because they don't think or feel like you, that doesn't mean that they are wrong. People typically do the best they can. Rarely do people intentionally set out to annoy others or create conflict. If somebody says or does something that makes you feel tension, take a step back and look as objectively as possible on the situation. Assume that they have positive intent.

If you only do one thing, let it be this one – *assume positive intent*. The positive intent may not be clear to you as you don't always have the full context or particular experience of the other person. However, just because it's not easy to grasp what the positive intention is, it's still fair to assume there is one.

Solution 4: Step into someone else's shoes

In order to really understand another person, you need to proactively find some way of stepping into their shoes. If your team members have a hard time seeing eye to eye, you can for example get them to try out each other's roles, simply swapping roles for a time, to gain greater understanding. You can also encourage or force team members to buddy up, especially those that don't work so well together. Reflect on this story that we recently heard:

> There was once a beautiful country, where everything was yellow in colour – sky, grass, buildings and people too. It wasn't necessarily that everything was yellow, but everything *appeared* yellow as people somehow looked at the world through yellow lenses. This was perfectly natural to them. They liked it, it was familiar and safe and good – and never questioned.
>
> One day a young woman started wondering what other countries there were to discover out there in the big world. She had heard about a blue land somewhere and she was intrigued by the idea of something different. She decided to go visit this strange, blue land.
>
> When she arrived she was given a pair of blue glasses, like everyone else. And with these on she explored and experienced this new, exciting country.
>
> When she finally travelled back home again, her friends all asked her: 'How was it?'
>
> 'It was great' she said 'and everything was wonderfully GREEN.'

As you can see – yes, we can step into someone else's shoes. And as you can also see, it's still going to be through our own lens that we take in someone's perspective. So it may not be entirely clear and objective, but it's still much more than we had before.

Solution 5: Connect up team members' goals

Every team needs goals, for the team as a whole and for the individuals. If you don't have them, go get them. Team members need to be included in the creation of the goals to get their commitment to them.

Make sure the goals are connected and support the work of the team. Connected goals are when team members each have a stake in each other's success. Connected goals mean that people are encouraged to work together to achieve results. It's not possible for one person to achieve individual success and leave the others behind.

Keep looking at the goals regularly, not just once or twice a year, to help the team deliver.

And to take it a step further, effective organisations have goals that are connected at all levels. Sometimes leaders higher up in the organisation push goals down, but the solution to avoiding conflict and tension is having synchronised goals. This is particularly important in matrix organisations where people may have multiple reporting lines that definitely create confusion unless addressed. If you don't have synchronisation, there will be tension. Make sure goals match and connect as much as possible. Even if there's not complete alignment, any improvement you can make will help. So keep checking the alignment of your goals, regularly. If you are not in a position to control it, then at least go and influence it.

Solution 6: Let go of the need to be right

We discussed earlier that conflict is merely a difference of opinion. No opinion is necessarily right or wrong, good or bad – it's just a different opinion. Your mindset makes the difference.

By letting go of the need to be right, you can consider the other opinion and watch the tension fade. Besides, based on the fast speed of change, what was appropriate before may no longer be. Research shows that half of what technical college students learn in their first year is already outdated by their third year.[3]

So what you think you are right about, you may not be. Keep an open mind.

Solution 7: Work on self-esteem

When people, consciously or unconsciously, experience self-doubt, they are more likely to react defensively and therefore feel internal tension and to create external tension with others. In the example of Sarah, her sense of inferiority in relationship to Rob made her unsure of herself and she felt she had to prove herself. In this instance it made her behave in a competitive manner. In other instances it might drive completely different behaviours, such as withdrawal or aggression. Self-esteem (belief in one's self-worth), drives how we behave.

One solution to minimising conflict and tension is therefore to work on your self-esteem. We all experience self-doubt or lower self-esteem at different times in our life, in different situations. We can have high self-esteem in certain areas and low in others, and this keeps changing. This is perfectly natural. Self-esteem is driven by how we think and feel (see 'Thoughts and feelings of team and leader' below).

Solution 8: Voice disagreement in a good way

If you voice disagreement in a good way, you can improve the results by really getting both of you to consider the various options. One way of doing this, is to avoid the word 'but' and replace it with 'and'. This builds bridges instead of walls between people.

Let's have a look at what Sarah and the other players could have done instead, had they deployed these solutions.

Interesting with this new guy Rob joining our team. It could have been awkward with him having worked with Harriet before, but she actually did a really good job at explaining why she had employed him. His IT background will make all the difference on the EXODUS project. It will

▶ *certainly make my life easier. It would be good to talk to Clark about Rob joining the team.*

Sarah sent an instant message to Clark and was pleased to find out that he was indeed available for a quick call.

Her phone shook as Clark's name appeared on its screen.

'Hi Clark!' she said, pleased to catch up.

After some initial pleasantries, she got to the subject she wanted to discuss.

'What do you think of Rob joining the team?'

'Why are you asking? Has he ruffled your feathers?' Clark responded with a smile in his voice.

Sarah smiled and retorted: 'No, not at all. I have to admit that I had some concerns at first, as I wasn't sure what his role was going to be. But I think Harriet very quickly made that clear. And it was great to have that meeting as soon as he had joined, where we all got a chance to get to know him a bit and understand more about his professional background.'

'Yes, it was a good meeting. I had some of the same thoughts as you actually. I wasn't quite sure about him at the beginning, but that helped.' Clark agreed.

'I have heard that Rob will be given the EXODUS project. I wanted this myself, but I guess it makes sense that he gets it, given his background, what do you think?'

'Yes, probably, although I can see that it would have suited you too. You can still help him though, can't you? You have experience he hasn't, but you can also learn from him, right? Besides, he's seems like a nice guy. He's probably good to work with.'

After the call, Sarah reflected on the conversation and was reassured by Clark's helpful and honest points.

It feels good to have that kind of open discussion with Clark. He and I always seem to be able to do that though, which maybe I don't with the others. I could probably make that happen with my other colleagues as well.

Behaviours of team and leader

Under 'Solutions' above, we have listed a number of 'how to' actions. These solutions work best when carried out with these supporting 'how to' behaviours. The actions on their own will get you only so far. With the right behaviours you can more effectively manage conflict and tension in the team.

'How to' solutions	'How to' behaviours	How the behaviours make the difference
Communicate, communicate, communicate.	Listening and caring (the desire to help people)	By listening, and understanding the person you are talking to, coupled with a genuine desire to help, you are able to not just convey data but also give it meaning that matters to that particular person.
Get together and ask constructive questions.	Being courageous Being sincere Being inventive Listening	When you have the courage to ask constructive questions, you demonstrate that it's OK to talk about difficult subjects. Courage breeds courage. Sincerity makes others feel that you really want to help. Asking questions in a listening and inventive way means you are finding the right questions for each person in a given situation.
Assume positive intent.	Being accepting Being curious	By being intentionally curious and accepting of others, it's easier to assume positive intent. Your mindset is shifted to a state where you want the best for the other person. You can then be more accepting of differing views.
Step into someone else's shoes.	Being curious Being thoughtful (thinking things over)	With curiosity and thoughtfulness, you can really start thinking about how others feel and how they may respond or react. When you step into someone else's shoes, you look at it through their lens, which means you can get better outcomes. Be aware of how automatic our responses are when we are looking at things through our own glasses.
Connect up team members' goals.	Being conscientious (taking the time to do things right)	When you're conscientious, you take the time and effort to properly connect team members' goals. This makes them feel connected to something bigger than themselves, which helps them understand what they are here to do every day as well as how they fit into the bigger purpose.

▶

'How to' solutions	'How to' behaviours	How the behaviours make the difference
Let go of the need to be right.	Being accepting Being curious	Think of someone that you know who always wants to be right. Just think of the impact it has on you! By being accepting and curious, it helps you to let go of any need to be right. It allows for other views to come in and perhaps develop an idea/solution into something greater than it would have been otherwise.
Work on self-esteem.	Being accepting (of self and others)	By being accepting, you can have a more positive view of yourself, which is a measure of 'how much you like yourself', your self-esteem. Working on your internal view of you helps you to work with others in a more open way. It allows you to behave in a more authentic way and be who you really are.
Voice disagreement in a good way.	Being respectful	Disagreements are OK and helpful, so position them in a positive way, treating the other person with respect. Think about HOW you are going to position the disagreement rather than what you are going to say. Spend time to think it through and think of the outcome you want to gain, which is win–win for all.

We've focused here on useful behaviours when it comes to resolving conflict and tension.

When intentionally practised over time, they become powerful, impactful habits that happen naturally.

Thoughts and feelings of team and leader

On average, a person experiences around 70.000 thoughts per day.[1]

Many of those thoughts are habits that affect a person's mindset or outlook.

> What we think affects how we feel, and how we feel affects how we think.

When wanting to manage and/or resolve conflict and tension within a team, actively replace thoughts and feelings that are counterproductive to that. Here are thoughts from the story, the impact they have on feelings and how they can be changed.

Negative thoughts	Negative feelings	Powerful thoughts	Powerful feelings
I don't feel comfortable around the new guy.	Nervousness Envy Animosity	*New is good. It will be great to see what the new guy will bring.*	Curiosity Hope
What is she playing at?	Suspicion	*I wonder what she wants to achieve here.*	Curiosity
How annoying that he didn't agree with me!	Anger	*OK, he's of a different opinion. Let's consider where that could take us.*	Curiosity Hope
What an idiot!	Anger Animosity	*We are clearly of different opinions. That's fine. It's not good, it's not bad – it just is.*	Understanding
Why don't they just see that I am right?	Anger Frustration	*I don't need to be right. Who's to say what's right or wrong anyway.*	Open-minded
I don't know why they are doing that.	Frustration Suspicion	*I am sure they are doing that for a reason. I'll talk to them about it and find out.*	Receptive
It should have been me!	Jealousy	*I'm sure there is a reason he/she was chosen for this. There will be other opportunities for me.*	Accepting
What's the point of that comment?	Suspicion	*Interesting comment. I want to know more.*	Confident

Summary

Conflict is simply a difference of opinion, which in and of itself is not bad. It's how we handle the conflict that makes the difference.

Healthy disagreement can lead to better ideas, greater insight; simply a smarter, more effective working environment.

Tension occurs when things are unclear and/or uncertain which makes people suspicious. Tension often leads to conflict and vice versa. They feed off each other.

The key solution to tension and conflict is of course communication.

Team communication

Communicate, communicate, communicate. It's almost not possible to over-communicate in a conflict situation. Communication provides clarity and as most tension and conflict is down to lack of clarity or misunderstanding, the solution is communication. Honest, respectful, curious communication.

In addition to this, *how* you approach a person who has different opinion will dictate the outcome, good or bad. Imagine that you are the leader of a team and one of your team members seems to be avoiding you; there is clearly some tension there. You could say, 'What's wrong with you?' or you could say, 'I was just wondering, how are you doing? We haven't had a chance to catch up for a while. Could we grab a coffee together?'

Which one would make you feel like opening up and dealing with the tension?

Team open-mindedness

Encourage team members to keep an open mind and see the other person's perspective. Let go of the need to be right! It's not right, it's not wrong, it just is. Go try that out! If you can create that in a team, it can grow to other departments and even start a culture of open mindedness.

And if you take only one thing from this chapter, let it be this: Assume positive intent!

Reflection questions for the reader

Look at your team and consider:

- ■ How open and honest is the communication between team members?
- ■ How clear are my team's roles and goals?

- How well aligned are our team's goals?
- To what extent am I keeping an open mind when others' views differ from mine?
- How am I voicing disagreements?
- How can I let go of the need to be right?

Self-assessment

After you have implemented the solutions in this chapter, answer these questions again to see the progress you have made.

How would you rate the following in your team?

	1 Very poor	2 Poor	3 Just OK	4 Good	5 Excellent
Communication					
Healthy Debating					
Constructive disagreement					
Open-mindedness					

3

How do you encourage everyone to share relevant information with each other?

- Increasing sharing of information
- Increasing sharing of wisdom
- Improving team learning

'The more we share, the more we have.'

Leonard Nimoy

Self-assessment

Before reading the chapter, do the following quick self-assessment.

How would you rate the following in your team?

	1 Very poor	2 Poor	3 Just OK	4 Good	5 Excellent
Sharing of knowledge					
Sharing of experience					
Collaboration					
Team spirit					

Competitors or colleagues?

Fernando and Carlos sat opposite each other. They were colleagues in a sales team. They worked independently and were both successful in their own regional areas. Their sales director, on the spur of the moment, had asked them to sit down and compare notes on their individual sales strategies.

Fernando sighed. 'OK, let's do this. We need to talk about our strategies, but I'm not sure what benefit that will give us, to be honest. We still have different regions that we're responsible for and I'm not sure what I'm doing is applicable where you are – and vice versa.' He looked at Carlos for agreement and as he didn't get a response, he felt confident and hence continued his one-way dialogue. 'Look, I know what I'm doing, I've been doing it for years. I don't actually need any help, I am however prepared to share some of my extensive experience, if needed.'

Fernando wasn't going to share anything more than what he absolutely needed to. *Why should I?* he thought. He had worked hard for his success and deep inside he was reluctant to just give that away

▶

to someone else, even if it was a colleague. In a way he felt hurt that his boss had even suggested this meeting. Besides, he didn't really see Carlos as a colleague, they were all competitors in his mind.

Carlos had watched Fernando with great interest through his monologue.

I always thought he was arrogant. And here we are, being asked to collaborate, and I'm not sure I want to. I came into this with an open mind but it's very obvious that he is not going to be forthcoming with his strategy, so I'll probably hold back too. Why should I share if he is not going to? Carlos was irritated by the whole situation.

With some hesitation they started exploring their sales accounts, and it turned into a 'look how great I am' display. As they were going down the list of existing clients, Fernando spotted the name of a company that he knew also existed in his region. In his mind, he decided to add them to his list of prospects, but didn't say anything to Carlos about it.

A month later Carlos was in a meeting with the customer in question. The customer was eager to speak:

'We were contacted by one of your colleagues, I think his name was Fernando,' he started.

Carlos tried not to look too surprised. He was suppressing his anger. His stomach started to churn.

'He contacted one of our other regional head offices, to sell your portfolio. I wanted to let you know that we were a bit surprised by this, but then we don't know how your company works. However, I'm sorry to say that we had to turn him down, because he just didn't seem to understand our needs well enough. I only found out afterwards, otherwise I would have put in a good word for your company, but as it now stands, the business in that region was given to one of your competitors. I'm sorry.'

Carlos was speechless. Not only had they lost the business, but the customer's perception of them had also been impacted. Carlos was furious. He was hit by an overwhelming sense of being let down. He was embarrassed. Carlos knew that he would have to pick up the phone and confront Fernando as soon as he left the meeting.

Exploring the problem

The two sales colleagues in the given example, are not collaborating, they are simply co-existing. And as a result, they miss out on a major sale, which affects both Fernando's sales results as well as the organisation's revenue.

Having team members who don't freely share what they know, is a challenge that most teams face, not just a sales team such as this one. Sometimes people don't make the link between lack of sharing and not getting as good a result as they could have. Let's explore this example in more depth to see what was going on.

Sharing

Fernando doesn't want to share what he knows. He's not used to doing it and he doesn't see any advantage in doing it. He feels like he has worked hard to get to where he is, and doesn't think that he should hand that experience over to others. He thinks they should have to work as hard for it as he has done. And given that he views his colleagues as competitors, it becomes very obvious why he won't give any information away. This mindset holds him back from any meaningful collaboration.

Fernando doesn't feel like he has anything to learn. With a long career in sales, Fernando is confident that he knows everything he needs to know about selling. He's not considering that Carlos could have other insights and knowledge, which he could benefit from. He feels superior to Carlos, but his behaviours are telling a different story.

Carlos won't share because Fernando won't share. Initially Carlos keeps an open mind to collaboration. But as Fernando is taking on a superior stance as well as showing his reluctance to sharing, Carlos withdraws from the opportunity of collaboration. He colludes with Fernando's behaviour by thinking, 'If you don't tell me, I won't tell you'. This almost child-like behaviour is played out time and time again in business.

Impact on productivity

By not having a meaningful and generous exchange of their sales strategies, Fernando and Carlos are less productive, as indicated by the loss of a sale.

In this example there is an obvious link between lack of sharing and the effect that has on the results. It's not always as obvious as this, which is why the importance of sharing is sometimes overlooked in teams and in organisations as a whole. But if we ignore sharing, then the cost to the business could be much more dramatic than we realise. To understand how to overcome this challenge, we need to first be aware of why people may not be forthcoming with information.

The reasons for not sharing relevant information in teams

Believing that knowledge is power

This is a common misperception. With this belief people will withhold information as they expect it will make them weaker if they give information away. However, the opposite is true. There is the old-fashioned saying that 'knowledge is power' yet today we live in a world where information is so quickly out of date that we need to share simply to keep up to date. We therefore need to acknowledge that on *some* occasions knowledge is power, however dysfunctional that might be.

Lack of awareness

If there is no habit of sharing, people won't share. They won't be used to it so they won't see it as important or even an option. They don't know what they don't know. They won't see the benefits of sharing as they haven't experienced it. If people are also busy, which many increasingly are, there will also not be any appetite for even taking the time out to try it and see what it could lead to.

Silo thinking

If people don't understand how what they are doing fits into the bigger picture, they will not see a reason for sharing as they will only be narrowly focused on their own part. They may be used to working alone and not have had reason to consider how this could help them or others.

Not valuing your own knowledge

If you don't value your own knowledge or opinion, you are less likely to think anyone else would either. This will mean you are not stepping forward to offer your contribution to a discussion or a collaborative situation.

Competitive thinking

If you see your colleagues as competitors, this will inevitably inhibit you from sharing. In a perceived competition, you compare yourself with others and will not share as it would give your 'competitors' an advantage they did not have before. It's driven from win–lose thinking where you think there can only be one winner.

Another aspect of competitive thinking, is making any sharing conditional. It's based on the underlying idea that you will only share something if you get something back. 'If you don't tell me, I won't tell you.'

Yet another expression of competitive thinking is to want others to have to work as hard for it as you have had to.

Fear-driven behaviours

It can feel scary to share. You may feel as if you are giving away something very valuable, and you may be fearful of what that does to your position in the team. It may make you question if you will still be as valuable when your knowledge has been spread to others.

Feeling threatened, whether the threat is real or perceived, drives defensive or at least protective behaviours.

Protection

In some cases, information is withheld in order to protect others. The logic behind this is that people may not be able to handle the information or may be hurt by it.

The impact of not sharing information/knowledge in teams

When information, knowledge and experience is not shared, it limits the intellectual bank of the team. The team cannot perform as effectively.

This is how a team is impacted:

- Duplication of work happens when people don't know what others are doing or how others could help through their knowledge. When information isn't flowing freely, there is a risk of continuously 'reinventing the wheel'. Someone could have solved the problem before but as their solutions are not readily shared, you end up doing the same thing again. Ultimately this creates a higher workload and makes people busier for no logical reason.

- There is less collaboration. People do their own thing, work in silos and are less likely to reach out to their colleagues. People are driven to work in silos.

- Learning is negatively impacted. When not sharing, you're taking away the other person's opportunity for learning and growth. The team's growth is therefore also affected.

- Team spirit is eroded when you know someone knows something and he/she is not sharing it. This affects the trust levels.

- Retaliating behaviour such as 'If you don't tell me, I won't tell you' brings down the maturity level of teamwork.

- The team is not achieving as much as it could. The collective intelligence of the team is not fully utilised.

The impact on the business, customers, employees and stakeholders

The example at the beginning of this chapter shows the impact on the business overall when information is not actively shared.

As highlighted with regards to team, the organisation overall is also affected through everyone being busier than needed, with unnecessary work overload and stress increasing the risk of avoidable mistakes.

Let's look at another example of business impact, this time with a focus on employees across the organisation.

Stella was cross about the latest reorganisation, which meant she now reported to Rajeev. Even though she respected him, they didn't have the best working relationship as she always felt as if he wanted to take over in meetings. She found him controlling. With her specialist knowledge of the bank, her participation in meetings and projects was crucial. She found herself withdrawing from any situations where she knew Rajeev would be, in order to stop him from attempting to control her. Stella also didn't want to give away too much of her expertise to him as she felt this would weaken her position. Stella had been with the bank for many years and Rajeev was relatively new. She quite liked having the upper hand and didn't want him to know more than her, which he would if she shared her business secrets with him.

Over time, her non-productive behaviour was noticed by others. She was seen as difficult to work with and hard to get any information out of. She started to become a problem. Whenever they could, her peers excluded her from meetings. She was becoming *the problem*. There were hushed conversations in the corridor and they were talking behind her back, saying how it would be easier to leave her out because it was just too much hassle getting valuable information out of her.

As this short story exemplifies, non-sharing behaviours create a work-around culture. This kind of culture is not effective, it wastes time and people start feeling unsettled. Engagement levels go down as does commitment and loyalty, and eventually people could leave. This all equates to a higher cost of doing business.

Because of this lack of sharing, customers can get mixed or conflicting messages as employees are not talking enough with each other. In the example of Fernando and Carlos, the customer is confused about how Carlos's company is operating. Their actions don't seem to join up in the eyes of the customer and this creates some quiet concern. This leaves the customer with a possible question mark over the continued relationship.

In this case, we can all observe the impact in the story. The question to ask yourself is this though: How many of these situations occur without you even being aware of them?

Solutions

Getting people to share information, knowledge, and experience is a crucial business opportunity not to be missed. What you are actually getting access to is wisdom.

Knowledge + Experience + Knowing what to do with it = Wisdom

'It is a characteristic of wisdom not to do desperate things.'
Henry David Thoreau

When there's a healthy flow of communication, you are creating a learning culture, where contributions multiply to the benefit of individual, team and organisations.

Let's get specific on how to do it.

Solution 1: It starts with you!

If you want others to share what they know, maybe even having worked hard to get to know, take the first step and role model the kind of sharing you want to see. Fearlessly share what you know, what you've experienced, what you've learned. Then ask people to do the same. Actions speak louder than words. Believe with conviction that it will make a difference, as people will sense your conviction and that impacts your results positively.

Solution 2: Make people aware of the effect

To convince anyone that it's worthwhile to open up and be generous, you need to explain why. Find examples of what happened when people did share and when people didn't. Give people feedback in the moment, real time, when this is happening. Tell them what you've observed and what impact it has on you, the team and the organisation. Suggest what to do next.

This TOP (Team, Organisation, Person) feedback model shows the process of effective feedback. This model demonstrates that you can give feedback by taking the observed behaviour and talking about the impact on the team, the organisation and you personally. Ensuring that you remain focused on the behavioural aspects.

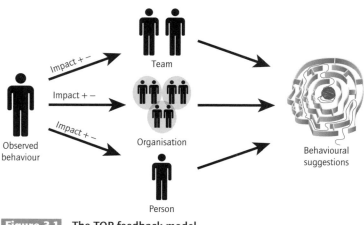

Figure 3.1   The TOP feedback model

To use this TOP feedback model in the team, follow these steps:

1. Think about the person's behaviour that you have observed.

2. Then think about the IMPACT those behaviours have on the team, the organisation and finally on you personally, with a specific focus on how it makes you feel.

3. Prepare your suggestion for what they could do going forward (this can of course be positively reinforcing a strength as well as something to do differently).

4. Then give the feedback to the person and listen to their thoughts on the subject.

If we use the example with Stella it may sound like this:

> Stella, what I really like about you is the wealth of experience you have on the bank, the business and the organisation, and when you DO share your experience I like your style of being open and honest.

It has an impact on the **team** because we have access to you and you can really help us with the challenges we face. You know all the relevant people and who to go to for what. I would like to see you share more of it with us.

Your experience is a great asset to the **organisation**. For me **personally,** I am happy with your knowledge and I really would like you to volunteer that information rather than me having to ask for it.

It would be good if you could share more and get involved more with the team.

Solution 3: Create and run 'sharing PODS'

Make it easy for people to share by creating specific sessions for this purpose. Create and run specific 'sharing PODS' where the participants are facilitated through a process of giving knowledge/experience input on a given subject. PODS sessions could be run for small and informal as well as big, more formal and complex purposes.

Power

Of

Dynamic

Sharing

Examples of this could include PODS sessions on how to retain customers or talent. Participants would be invited to come prepared to share examples of what has worked and what hasn't worked from their experience.

Solution 4: Link to the big picture

Take a look at the big picture with your team. Identify where you fit in the overall picture of the organisation. Start by considering the following questions:

- How does the work you do contribute to the purpose of the organisation?
- Who is dependent on your work?
- Who are you dependent upon to be able to deliver?

Understanding where your team fits in the success chain, needs to be part of your culture. This kind of ongoing discussion creates a heightened level of social awareness and makes people look up and look around them.

Solution 5: Celebrate successes of when it's worked and delivered results

Make the case for generous, fearless sharing by noticing when it happens and recognising people for doing it. Give individuals credit for their generosity and celebrate the results it leads to. Be specific and point to cause and effect, e.g. 'This person took time to update you all on what he had learnt in a process improvement workshop, and as a result we have all become more aware of process improvement opportunities and have managed to cut the verification process time in half. This has affected client satisfaction as well as allowing us to take on more clients, and increasing revenue.'

Force yourself as a team to stop and celebrate success.

Solution 6: Dare to share

Sharing doesn't always come easy. It can feel scary, but as Susan Jeffers so clearly stated in her book with the same name: 'Feel the Fear – and do it anyway'.[4] Sometimes you just have to be brave and step out of your comfort zone to make new things happen.

Let's have a look at what Fernando and Carlos could have done instead, had they deployed these solutions.

> Fernando and Carlos sat opposite each other. Their sales director, on the spur of the moment, had asked them to sit down and compare notes on their individual sales strategies.
>
> Fernando looked at Carlos and confessed. 'OK, I have to admit that I was a bit hesitant about this. I'm not sure what benefit it will give us, but I'm willing to give it a shot. In a way, we've almost worked

▶

▶ as competitors for all these years, competing for the sales champion titles.' Fernando smiled wryly. 'Actually, when I put it that way, it sounds a bit crazy what we've been doing, we ARE colleagues after all.' He paused and then continued: 'What do you think?' He looked inquiringly at Carlos.

Carlos had watched Fernando with great interest through his monologue.

Hmm. This is turning out more interesting than I would have thought. Fernando is more open-minded than I would have previously given him credit for. I came into this with an open mind and it looks like he did too. Interesting, this might create all sorts of new opportunities. Carlos was beginning to feel more optimistic.

'I agree,' Carlos responded. 'I know we all have our own tricks of the trade and we've always kept them to ourselves. But maybe he is right, maybe we can achieve more by sharing those tricks. I'm happy to give it a go. It's not like we are really competing with each other after all. But it's a very different way of thinking, that's for sure!' Carlos scratched his head with bemusement.

With some hesitation they started exploring their sales accounts, and as they were going down the list of Carlos' existing clients, Fernando spotted the name of a company that he knew also existed in his region. He turned to Carlos and said, 'Wow, look at that. I didn't know you had them. I have been considering contacting them for my region. What do I need to know about them? What can you tell me about them?'

A month later Carlos was in a meeting with the customer in question. The customer was eager to speak: 'We were contacted by one of your colleagues, I think his name was Fernando,' he started.

'He contacted one of our other regional head offices, to sell your portfolio. And apparently he did a great job at it, because your company now also has that region. This together with the fact that I have long since sung your praises, has now made our CEO want to discuss signing a national contract. If the price is right, of course. Who do I talk to about that?' Carlos couldn't stop the smile from spreading across his face.

Behaviours of team and leader

Under 'Solution' above, we have listed a number of 'how to' actions. These solutions work best when carried out with these supporting 'how to' behaviours. The actions on their own will get you only so far. With the right behaviours you will get team members to share more effectively.

'How to' solutions	'How to' behaviours	How the behaviours make the difference
It starts with you!	Being courageous Being socially aware	In sharing your wisdom, you show both courage and generosity. You're also showing that the other party is important enough to share with. You demonstrate that you value them. By being socially aware, you understand the people you want to share with, so you know what knowledge is appropriate and relevant to share, and what you will elicit in others to share.
Make people aware of the effect.	Being honest Being respectful	When you tell people 'as it is' in a non-threatening way, it becomes obvious that it's for the greater good. You help people see that they can get a better result if they share. Once they've experienced it, they gain insight of its value and then will want to do more of it.
Create and run 'sharing PODS.	Being inventive Being curious Being encouraging	Through encouragement and openness, the 'sharing PODS' become a safe place to exchange knowledge, wisdom and experience. It opens up people's minds and ideas can flow and something greater can be created than if sharing hadn't happened.
Link to the big picture.	Being socially aware Being interested Being thoughtful	If you take a genuine interest in the organisation as a whole, you can more easily reflect on how what you are doing contributes to the overall purpose of the organisation. It creates an awareness of being involved in something bigger and therefore more powerful.
Celebrate successes of when sharing has worked and delivered results.	Being positive Being enthusiastic Being appreciative	When effective sharing is recognised and celebrated from the heart, it makes people feel valued. It gives you permission to take pride in what you've achieved. It's showing that it's OK to not just intellectually appreciate the results, but actually feel the excitement of it, which makes you want to do it again, to get that feeling again. And this is infectious for other people.

▶

'How to' solutions	'How to' behaviours	How the behaviours make the difference
Dare to share.	Being courageous	When you are fearful of sharing information because you believe you may lose power by doing so, and you still go ahead and do it, you grow. You realise that it worked and that you're still OK and that you've grown. By stepping out of your comfort zone you have expanded your experience and you now have a larger comfort zone from which to operate. You have a new level of understanding and it propels you to do more.

Thoughts and feelings of team and leader

On average, a person experiences around 70.000 thoughts per day.[1]

Many of those thoughts are habits that affect a person's mindset or outlook.

What we think affects how we feel, and how we feel affects how we think.

When wanting to share information within a team, actively replace thoughts and feelings that are counterproductive to that. Here are thoughts from the story and some additional ones, their impact on feelings and how they can be changed.

Negative thoughts	Negative feelings	Powerful thoughts	Powerful feelings
Why should I share more than what I absolutely need to?	Animosity Fear	*If I learn then maybe others will too, and I will get something out of it as well.*	Curiosity Hope
I always thought he was arrogant.	Annoyance	*He is strong-minded, I knew that. And probably proud too, and that's good – I can sympathise with that.*	Acceptance Sense of kinship
Why should I share if he is not going to?	Irritation	*Maybe if I start sharing, he'll do it too.*	Curiosity Hope

▶

Negative thoughts	Negative feelings	Powerful thoughts	Powerful feelings
Why should I give away my hard-earned experience?	Defensiveness	*He's worked hard too. We all do. Are there things we can learn from each other?*	Generosity Sense of openness
What I know is nothing special.	Self-doubt	*I actually know quite a lot that can be of value to others.*	Pride Achievement
I will just do my own thing, regardless of what they are doing.	Selfish Fearful	*I will reach out, it just doesn't make sense to not work together. I don't want to reinvent the wheel.*	Being brave Mutual respect

Summary

Teams are made up of individuals who all bring their unique set of skills, knowledge, experience and wisdom to the table.

Fearlessly share

Effective teams are those who regularly, generously and fearlessly share what they know for the benefit of everyone. In order for this to happen, there needs to be a good level of trust.

Powerful sharing

An effective way of building trust is to kick off some powerful sharing, starting small and building it up. Then actively and explicitly explain the links to why the sharing made a difference and where. It could be as simple as a debrief meeting or discussion after a meeting, simply saying 'let's share what worked here and what didn't work'. Take the first step and start sharing more than you did yesterday and just watch the results.

Reflection questions for the reader

Look at your team and consider:

- How much sharing goes on in the team?
- Do people hold on to specialist knowledge?

■ How could we create more opportunities for formal and informal sharing?

■ How am I a role model for information sharing?

■ How much success are we celebrating?

Self-assessment

After you have implemented the solutions in this chapter, answer these questions again to see the progress you have made.

How would you rate the following in your team?

	1 Very poor	2 Poor	3 Just OK	4 Good	5 Excellent
Sharing of knowledge					
Sharing of experience					
Collaboration					
Team spirit					

How do you create engagement?

- Increasing team engagement
- Increasing team self-esteem

'Tell me and I'll forget. Show me and I may remember. Involve me and I'll understand.'

Chinese proverb

Self-assessment

Before reading the chapter, do the following quick self-assessment.

How would you rate the following in your team?

	1 Very poor	2 Poor	3 Just OK	4 Good	5 Excellent
Overall engagement					
How good the team feels about itself (team self-esteem)					
Celebrating successes					

The same old story

> Roger was bored. He stifled a yawn and his eyes travelled across the room without really noticing any of his colleagues around the table. If it had been up to him, he wouldn't have been there. In his mind, this was just another pointless exercise of a bunch of people getting together. He had told them all before so why did he need to repeat it or listen to them talk about it again. Roger was in charge of one of the big IT projects and was always one step ahead of everyone. He was very bright and found it frustrating having to explain his thinking to his peers, who in his mind clearly were not as bright and simply didn't understand his world. *They never would*, he thought.
>
> Felicity, the marketing manager was getting very annoyed with him now, as indicated by her sharp tone. 'Roger, why don't you explain to us *again* why we are so behind with this IT installation. The deadlines are being missed, I just don't understand why this is happening.'
>
> Roger quickly turned his head towards Felicity, a little too quickly, shooting her a steely glare. He fired his response 'I have told you before and *once again* I will tell you that we have not been getting

▶

the cooperation from your teams in following through our requests for information, they just don't respond quickly enough.'

Felicity raised her eyebrows. 'And I have told *you,* if we don't know when you are going to send the requests and we don't understand why *and* have some involvement in that, we cannot help you. In any case I didn't know you were *still* waiting for that information, why didn't you come to me?' She folded her arms and sat back demonstratively.

The last thing Roger wanted to do was to have more to do with Felicity's team. His leader was always asking him to involve his peers and keep them updated. Roger was tired of hearing that same message repeated. In his mind that would just slow things down, and they didn't have the time if they were going to meet the final implementation deadline. Besides, all he had asked for was some additional information from Felicity's team. It wasn't that complicated. *They just need to keep up*, he thought to himself.

'I assumed you knew. Regardless, this is the reason we are in danger of not meeting those targets. So I suggest we leave it there and just go with what we've got. I'll contact you if we need any other information from you.' Roger nodded that he had finished and walked out, while muttering something about being late for another meeting.

Felicity felt despondent and tired. This kind of discussion had gone on so many times before and it drained her. *I am not going to help him anymore.* She found herself withdrawing from her team of peers.

Exploring the problem

Global studies repeatedly indicate that less than a fifth of employees are fully engaged at work and this is a massive waste of human capital on behalf of the company and just as importantly a waste of people's time. According to Gallup, there are three types of employees: Engaged, Not Engaged and Actively Disengaged. [5]

Team members who are not engaged, are not particularly interested, they can even be apathetic. They are there in body, but not mentally or emotionally.

Those that are actively disengaged are openly showing how unhappy and disenchanted they are.

In the story, both Roger and Felicity are showing signs of not being engaged, for different reasons. Roger is bored with having to explain what to him is very obvious. Felicity feels like an order taker rather than someone who is invited to participate. She considers the requests to be very disjointed as she's not been included in the ongoing discussions. As a result, they both withdraw their engagement from the team and the project.

When people are not fully engaged, they are, whether they know it or not, not valuing their own time enough to stay engaged and make the most of any situation they are in.

The reasons for lack of engagement, or even apathy

Boredom

If a person is bored, they switch off, they slow down and they lack energy. Boredom has different drivers, such as not seeing the point in something or the reason for it. It can also be because they don't understand the bigger reason for doing it, the bigger picture. Another reason for boredom is when a person perceives their job to be boring, either in content, context or environment. That kind of tedium can also specifically relate to a job where the person feels unable to innovate or think differently about their job and how it is performed. Overly repetitive work can cause disinterest and apathy.

Not feeling important

If it's not obvious to people how they add value to the organisation, they won't think they are important. They may not feel either seen or heard. For whatever reason, their contribution is not getting enough attention from their leader or other relevant people around them. They are not getting enough feedback on their work or the value they bring. By not being noticed, they are not receiving recognition and there can be no celebration when results are achieved. In the story, Felicity is interpreting her not being invited to play an active part in the project, as an indication that she is only being an order taker and not as important as her peer. Also in the story, Roger is annoyed that he should have to think about the impact on his peers and keep them informed. His boss is always talking about it but Roger is not realising the effect this could have.

Holding a grudge

Whenever team members hold a serious grudge against their boss or another person, or the organisation as a whole, they are engaging more with the grudge than their work. This could be a conscious choice, but it could also be completely subconscious/automatic. The *grudge* gets most of their focus – it's hard to hold a grudge AND be focused on your work. When there's a grudge against the organisation, the person will usually come to work anyway but they've effectively checked out and are probably doing the minimum they can get away with, which affects team members and team results.

Disillusionment

In the story Felicity is checking out, she is jaded by this conversation having happened so many times before. She is losing the will to continue to invest in the same dialogue again. This jaded feeling can lead to team members being disillusioned and disengaged.

Career stagnation

Career stagnation can be another reason for people to disengage. They have been in the role for too long, or they don't see any progression opportunities. Some team members can feel this way if they didn't get promoted and were not given effective feedback along with the reasons *why* they were not promoted.

Lack of control

If people don't feel in control of their own situation or don't feel consulted, it can impact their level of team engagement. If they think they can't impact their own situation it encourages them to withdraw and disconnect. They have a sense of not being in control. If this happens, they may get into a downward spiral of believing they can't do a good job so they stop trying. In the example Roger wants to be in control and Felicity feels she is not in control, which forces her to withdraw, particularly as this has happened many times before.

Uncelebrated success

This is something that is very common in teams where there is a lack of engagement, that there are leaders who don't take time to celebrate because they are too busy, or just busy getting on to the next thing. They don't stop to celebrate as they don't think it's a big deal. Also, they may not celebrate success because they don't feel what they have done is good enough or that it is just as expected. This feeling of 'not being good enough' or just having done what was expected leads to not being proud of achievements.

The impact of lack of engagement in teams

Lack of engagement is very apparent to other people, people don't have to SAY anything. The lack of engagement is obvious so negative impact is inevitable:

- It's contagious, it can spread like a virus. It's hard to stay engaged in a team if you are sitting next to someone who isn't. Imagine the impact of several disengaged colleagues.

- It creates resentment. Team members may get annoyed with those who aren't engaged and carrying their part of the workload. This results in uneven workload.

- Low engagement in a team doesn't feel good. The team will find it hard to feel good about itself – there will be lower team self-esteem.

- When team members are low in engagement, it's not enjoyable to work there – and employee turnover is therefore a great risk. Sadly, you are at more risk of losing those who have potential to be engaged, as they will not accept working in a non-engaging environment. And turnover is costly; hiring new people and bringing them to a high-performing level takes time and money – and can impact the customers' experience.

■ Negative retention – when people who are not engaged stay, this is costly too, as it affects several business success factors: team morale, customer experience, productivity and profitability.

The impact on the business, customers, employees and stakeholders

Employee engagement drives customer engagement, which in turn drives revenue. This is not something to take lightly.

Let's look at an example of the impact on customers.

> A company's finance department had experienced internal conflict for quite some time, which had not been properly dealt with by any of the people involved. One of the accountants was so hurt and angry that she could not properly focus on her job. She was more engaged in her anger and looking at what her colleagues were doing or not doing, than she was in her own job. She started making mistakes in her job, which included not paying out customer credits on time, which in turn affected one of the biggest clients several times. Eventually the client got tired of the bad treatment and removed their business from the company.

This example shows how dangerous lack of employee engagement can be on many levels, affecting productivity, customer experience and profitability.

An organisation pays for 100 per cent of employees' agreed working time. If employees are not fully engaged, the organisation is only getting a limited amount of their time and therefore their capability. Let's get specific. According to Gallup, 87 per cent of employees worldwide are not fully engaged at work. This means organisations are only getting full payback on 13 per cent of their investment in employee time and capability. [5]

The link to the bottom line is dramatic. If an employee is disengaged in a team, the viral effect means it is harder for others to be engaged too. Disengagement means that team members don't operate at the level of efficiency that they are capable of and, therefore, only perform a limited amount of work. An example is during times of change when as much as two hours per day can be made up by people simply talking about the change rather than doing their work. Imagine a team of ten people talking, not doing their job for two hours per day – that's a total of 20 hours per day. This has an impact on productivity as well as the customer experience (longer response times, etc.) and therefore profitability.

Solutions

To be engaged in a team environment means to feel committed to the team mission, to want to get involved and do your very best. It also means to feel motivated to 'go the extra mile'. You behave as if you are the owner of the mission, the team task, rather than a passive observer. You express enthusiasm in your behaviour as well as your word.

You feel connected and driven to do a good job. This positive effect is communicated to team members and becomes infectious in a positive way.

The team leader needs to have their 'engagement radar' on and assess how engaged the members are at any given time. This is not to say that team engagement is only the leader's responsibility of course. Everyone is ultimately responsible for how they spend and value their own time.

Let's get specific on how to do it.

Solution 1: Role-model personal response-ability

If you want others to be engaged, you need to start with yourself and find your motivation to give it your all. Anything can happen at work, sometimes good, sometimes bad. And whatever happens you have the *ability* to choose your *response* to that – you are *response-able.* By role-modelling that engagement is indeed in your own hands and not subject to external factors, you demonstrate to others that it's possible to stay engaged even when faced with challenges. It may not always feel like you have a choice at that particular point, but you do. Take a moment and ask yourself how you could respond to what has happened and remind yourself that you value your own time enough to make sure your choice is productive – and engagement is more productive than disengagement.

Figure 4.1 Response-ability

Solution 2: Clearly communicate the team's purpose and everyone's role in it

Talk with the team as a whole about what they, as a group, are here to do. Have an in-depth conversation about it so that each person can clearly see what it means to him/her personally, so they can connect to their job purpose not just in their head but in their heart too. Make sure there are opportunities to ask questions, discuss and get clarification.

Solution 3: Tell people how they are doing

Without feedback, people are flying blind. They need to know how they are doing. They need to know what they're doing well and what they can do better. Some people can figure this out themselves, but most people have blindspots and feedback can help with these. It's often easier to assess if you have completed a task but harder to assess *how* you did and what the impact was on the team, the organisation and maybe even the customer.

As a leader, you need to give regular feedback to each person as well as to the team. If it's good, tell them. If it's not good, help them work on how to develop in order to make it better. Make it part of the team's DNA as well, by including the following feedback points in each team meeting:

- What have we done since we last met that has worked well? Why has it worked well? What's been the impact?
- What have we done since we last met that has NOT worked well? Why has it NOT worked well? What's been the impact?

Solution 4: Get members working on innovative new ways of doing the job

Have a brainstorming session on how to invigorate the job. This could and should include questioning processes that don't add value, responsibility overlaps, process handovers and particularly time-consuming tasks. Use these questions to help drive innovation forward:

- What could we change to make the job more interesting/fun?
- Are we doing things that are repetitive and boring and bring very little value? If so, could they be stopped/changed/improved?
- If possible, what could we stop doing? What could we start doing? What should we continue doing?
- Could any tasks be swapped between team members (a new task owner can bring new perspective/ideas)?

In order to make the session productive for everyone, send out the questions in advance to allow reflection time ahead of the meeting for those who want it.

Solution 5: Be genuinely interested in your team members

Take an interest in each team member and the work they do by really listening to their ideas, concerns and interest. Find something in each person that you can be genuinely interested in. Make it authentic. When interest is truly authentic it sends a different message; the other person feels valued and important; they feel seen and heard as a person, not just a work contributor. They are seen as a whole person.

Solution 6: Have ongoing development discussions

Don't wait until the yearly appraisal. Have regular one-to-ones and make them truly two-way. Together, discuss how further development could happen. Don't feel like you have to have all the answers here. Be creative about development, it doesn't have to be a promotion or even a new same-level job, it could just be a new challenge that gives the added injection of engagement.

Encourage one-to-ones between team members too, as peer coaching can be a very powerful addition to someone's development.

Solution 7: Celebrate success

When things go well, you absolutely need to recognise and celebrate that. Stop and reflect on a regular basis, to recognise what's been done, what learning has happened and what has been achieved. You could do this individually and as a team. To make it into a habit, put reflection time into your calendar weekly. It doesn't have to be more than five or ten minutes, which is time everyone should be able to afford to invest. Take the time to celebrate too. Engage your team in *how* to celebrate (ask them!): coffee huddle, drinks, dinner, event, trip etc. It can be as small or as big as you want, but it must happen. And let's be honest, celebrating is fun, so let's just enjoy it.

Solution 8: Make it contagious

Attitudes and moods are contagious. Keep this in mind when you interact with your team. If you are disengaged, chances are you will find yourself in the company of others who are too. It's even more contagious than that. Just thinking about or discussing disengagement is disengaging! You are much better off focusing on how to engage, making *engagement* infectious.

Solution 9: Build team self-esteem

Just like an individual, a team can have varying levels of self-esteem.

When a team enjoy working together, is able to do a good job and its members are seen as important, the team will feel good about itself – it will have high team self-esteem.

Building team self-esteem is a way of increasing engagement in a team, and it's done through role modelling of personal response-ability, clarity of purpose, performance feedback, development discussions, innovative ways of doing the job, genuine interest, celebrating success and making it contagious.

Let's have a look at what Roger and Felicity could have done instead, had they deployed these solutions.

Roger stopped outside the meeting room. He needed to give himself a few minutes to think about how he wanted to behave in this meeting. Roger hadn't been looking forward to it. He was also rushing from meeting to meeting and he was a little frustrated because he knew he would have to explain the same thing all over again.

He stopped, took a deep breath, gave himself a moment, and it was only a moment, to reframe his thoughts for this meeting to get himself a better result. In a calmer, better frame of mind he pushed open the door, putting a smile on his face and nodding as he made eye contact with everyone around the table.

Felicity, the marketing manager, was annoyed with Roger, as indicated by her sharp tone. 'Roger, why don't you explain to us *again* why we are so behind with this IT installation. The deadlines are being missed, I just don't understand why this is happening.'

Roger was ready, as he knew he would need to explain himself again. Roger slowly turned to look at Felicity, taking the time to ensure he had her attention and was facing her. 'Felicity, I understand your frustration with this and I would like to talk to you in more detail about exactly what I need from your team. We haven't had time to take you through all of the stages and how your team fit in, so can we do that in the next few days? I would appreciate your support.' Roger was calm. 'I think there is some more information we need and I am sure that once we have it that will help us move much quicker towards that deadline.'

Felicity shrugged her shoulders and looked at her boss for some kind of reassurance, Felicity and Roger's boss nodded back at Felicity and gestured to say *carry on*.

'Yes, well if my team are holding us up then I can meet with you as soon as possible, I have some space tomorrow, can we make that work?' said Felicity.

Roger responded immediately. 'Yes that works for me, I also wanted to thank your team for some of the good work they have already put into the project. They seem to be trying hard. I just think we need to give

> you some better understanding of the bigger picture and what we are trying to achieve.'
>
> Felicity felt a sense of relief, there was a way forward and Roger had handled it well. She was ready to support him and was eager to get the meeting set up for tomorrow.

Behaviours of team and leader

Under 'Solutions' above, we have listed a number of 'how to' actions. These solutions work best when carried out with these supporting 'how to' behaviours. The actions on their own, will get you only so far. With the right behaviours you can more effectively create employee engagement.

'How to' solutions	'How to' behaviours	How the behaviours make the difference
Role-model personal *response-ability*.	Being positive	Whatever happens, whatever results you get, a positive outlook will increase your chances of finding something constructive to focus on to get a better result – and maintain engagement.
Clearly communicate the team's purpose and everyone's role in it.	Being inspiring Being conscientious	With inspiration you convey honest conviction in what you're communicating, so that others can get your message at the emotional level, not just at the intellectual level of words. By also being conscientious you take the time and care that's needed to ensure each person commits to his/her part in the purpose.
Tell people how they are doing.	Being sincere Being caring	By being caring and sincere in your feedback, you are more likely to have the other person not just listen to you but actually take on board the feedback and have the desire to change or maintain the behaviours needed for their success.
Get members working on innovative new ways of doing the job.	Listening Being curious Being open-minded	When listening with an open, curious mind, you are showing others that you value their ideas. But that's not all, you're also acknowledging that they can think creatively, which can help them to open up and break free from any limitations they may have about their ability to be creative. As a result, they will do it more.

'How to' solutions	'How to' behaviours	How the behaviours make the difference
Be genuinely interested in your team members.	Active listening	Genuine interest can be displayed in different ways, but usually requires some serious active listening where you let the other person know that you are finding what they have to say of interest. This is done through words of acknowledgement as well as facial expressions, nods, body posture, eye contact and tone of voice.
Have ongoing development discussions.	Being trustworthy Being caring	When you care enough about a team member and their career, you faithfully keep development discussion appointments, thereby showing the importance of these. Your focus is on what they need and want for themselves, not necessarily what you want for them.
Celebrate success.	Being positive Being enthusiastic	Get excited about celebration! If it's to be celebrated, your enthusiasm will make others feel that it's worth celebrating and that it's OK to think that what people have achieved is good.
Make it contagious.	Being enthusiastic	Whatever you do, impacts the experience of others. This is also true for engagement or lack thereof. Being enthusiastic, without going over the top, reflects your engagement and helps you to make your engagement contagious.
Build team self-esteem.	Being considerate Being conscientious	By being considerate you passionately want the best for your team, which means you want the team to do well and feel good about itself. By being conscientious, you make it happen, you don't give up – and that in itself makes the team members feel engaged.

Thoughts and feelings of team and leader

On average, a person experiences around 70.000 thoughts per day. [1]

Many of those thoughts are habits that affect a person's mindset or outlook.

What we think affects how we feel, and how we feel affects how we think.

When wanting to increase engagement within a team, actively replace thoughts and feelings that are counterproductive to that. Here are some thoughts from the story, their impact on feelings and how they can be changed.

Negative thoughts	Negative feelings	Powerful thoughts	Powerful feelings
... another pointless exercise of a bunch of people getting together.	Bored Hopeless	I believe this meeting can be useful and I intend to make it so!	Hope
I had told them all before, so why do I need to repeat it or listen to them talk about it again?	Irritation Indignation	I will make sure I am clearer this time, so that we can move ahead and get the things done that we need to.	Determination Optimism
... clearly they are not as bright and simply don't understand my world. They never would.	Arrogance	I have clearly not communicated this well enough, as they are not understanding it. I need to hold the mirror up to myself.	Responsibility Optimism
I don't want to be treated like an order taker.	Indignation Anger	OK, they need my help. I will help and see what we can do to change this for the better longer term.	Hope 'We are on the same side'
They just need to keep up.	Frustration	I need to help them keep up. Let's see what I can do.	Helpful
I am not going to help him anymore.	Defiance	We're in this together. I will help him and make sure this works – for both of us.	Helpful Hope

Summary

Team engagement is not just a 'nice to have', it's a driver of success.

Feeling connected

Team members who are engaged are interested in what they do. They are committed to the team mission, to 'going the extra mile'. They behave as if they are the owner of the mission, the team task, rather than a passive observer. They express enthusiasm in behaviour as well as words. They feel connected and driven to do a good job.

They are there in body, as well as mentally and emotionally. And this kind of behaviour is contagious.

Involvement

The key to engagement is involvement. By involving others, you make it impossible for them to stay detached. You are also demonstrating that they are paramount to the work the team does, which is also hard for them *not* to connect with.

Everyone's responsibility

Team engagement is everyone's responsibility. Each team member needs to have their 'engagement radar' on and assess how engaged they are themselves at any given time. Everyone is ultimately responsible for how they spend and value their own time, and being engaged is a way of valuing your time.

Reflection questions for the reader

- Does my team believe in the team's ability to achieve its purpose? Does my team have high team self-esteem?
- How often do I, as a team member or leader, change or cancel development discussions? And what's the impact of that, on me and others?
- What impact am I having on my team members through my actions and behaviours?
- How often do I innovate at work? How and when do I discuss new ways of doing things?

Self-assessment

After you have implemented the solutions in this chapter, answer these questions again to see the progress you have made.

How would you rate the following in your team?

	1 Very poor	2 Poor	3 Just OK	4 Good	5 Excellent
Overall engagement					
How good the team feels about itself (team self-esteem)					
Celebrating successes					

5

How do you create transparency and openness?

- Increasing transparency between team members within the team and with others
- Increasing levels of openness across the team and into the organisation

'No legacy is so rich as honesty.' William Shakespeare

Self-assessment

Before reading the chapter, do the following quick self-assessment.

How would you rate the following in your team?

	1 Very poor	2 Poor	3 Just OK	4 Good	5 Excellent
Transparency and openness					
Trust					
Courage to tell the truth					
Living the values					

George, the angry CEO

George, the CEO, had a temper. His volatility was well known and created a certain cautiousness when people were around him.

Noel didn't know how to break the news to George that he was £500K below their forecasted revenue. This was due to an incorrect prediction, which had only just been noticed by Noel. As George was known for 'shooting the messenger' when bad news hit, Noel didn't really want to be the one who got shot. George would behave very aggressively when anyone came to him with bad news. Noel needed to tell him there had been an error in the numbers that they couldn't fix, but he didn't dare. He decided to leave it until next month, hoping that it would somehow miraculously resolve itself. The next month it was £1 million, so much worse, and he knew he should do something so he went to talk to Theresa, another senior member of the team.

Theresa looked serious as Noel finished his story.

'Yes, this should be addressed, but maybe it could wait a bit longer. You know, just as I do, how much George has on his plate right now with the takeover looming. He's preoccupied and he is not very

▶

receptive to anything that's not directly related to that. I also wonder if the numbers could still improve as the last month is trending more positively. Given that George is such hard work, you may get into trouble unnecessarily. You saw how he ripped Tom apart at the quarterly review last week, didn't you?'

Theresa's question needed no answer and she fuelled Noel's fear and made him convinced that it would be more prudent to wait again.

'Yes, you are probably right. He is a bit of a tyrant, isn't he? Tom *did* try to tell him in a really good way and he had reasonable arguments, and George's response just shut everyone down. Did you notice how uncomfortably quiet it went after that?'

'Yes, I did. I felt myself wanting to melt into the background. I mean, who wants to be the next target after such a public dressing down! Hmm, I wonder if he has any idea what effect his outbursts have on others. Does he think it makes him powerful to behave like that? Well, it doesn't. He may shut people up, but he doesn't get the truth and he doesn't look like a great leader.'

Noel had to agree. It was becoming increasingly hard to work with George.

Well guess what; the next month it was £2 million and hiding was no longer an option for Noel. With a heavy heart he walked the corridor to George's office with his imaginary armour on, getting ready for an angry confrontation.

The predicted explosion occurred and George demanded to know why Noel hadn't come forward with this information sooner.

Noel mumbled something about trends and changing markets and not worrying George unnecessarily, none of which was particularly well received.

As he left the office, exhausted from the exchange, he was amazed that George didn't understand why he hadn't been approached before. *Well, I'm certainly not going to tell him, but somebody needs to!*

Exploring the problem

In the example, Noel is fearful of telling his CEO the truth about the budget. From a rational perspective he understands that he should speak up, but his fear pushes the logic away. With Theresa's help he even finds reasonable excuses not to tell George. This only delays the inevitable, i.e. talking to George, which makes George's reaction even stronger when Noel finally does talk to him.

Feeling threatened

George's anger is caused by him feeling threatened, threatened by the possibility of him looking bad as a leader if the budget is not met. By being defensive, he hinders any sensible conversation that could have been had. He points a finger at the messenger thereby making the messenger defensive, closing down any potential solutions.

And if it's a recurring event, it creates a very non-transparent culture of 'cover my a**e', where everyone defensively looks out for their own interests.

Fear

By not telling George directly, but instead going behind his back to Theresa, Noel is unwittingly creating a ripple effect of fear and non-transparency. Others will hear the story and think twice before approaching George with bad news.

George is at times a very fun and inspiring leader, but his occasional outbursts make his behaviours inconsistent. This causes people to not feel at ease with him as they don't know what his reaction will be. George is therefore in danger of surrounding himself with only 'yes-sayers', fearful of challenging him or bringing him bad news.

The reasons for people not being transparent and open

Don't dare to tell the truth

Fear of punishment or backlash can stop people from telling the truth, just like Noel in the story.

Don't think others can handle the truth or want to hear it

They may know from previous experience that the other person won't listen to the reality, so they withhold that nugget, thinking that it will be easier not to tell them the truth.

Not being heard by leader

If a leader is not listening to people or taking in their views, people will stop providing that input as it's not perceived as valued or welcomed. In the story, Theresa suggests not talking to George due to his preoccupation with a takeover, thinking that Noel wouldn't be heard anyway.

Don't want to be blamed

Blame is not a good word; no one wants to be blamed. But if they have been blamed a few times, it will stop them from putting themselves in the firing line. They will worry that their remuneration or career prospects may be negatively impacted, so they won't be keen to share information that isn't positive, thinking they might get a finger pointed at them.

No other outlet

As shown in the story, if we avoid talking directly to the relevant person and go elsewhere, it becomes gossip. Noel went to Theresa as he desperately needed an outlet, which is natural, as he didn't feel he could go to George. The act of talking behind someone's back though, which is what gossip effectively is, makes other people wonder when they will be talked about in the same way. A culture of gossip is born.

No culture of transparency

If talking openly about things, including issues, is not the norm, it will take focus and courage to break with that tradition.

Cultural differences

In an increasingly global workplace, different national/regional cultures can have different views on transparency. What's OK to be open about in one culture, could be potentially damaging in another. One such example is feedback: in some countries it's OK to give open and honest feedback to your manager, whereas in others it is not. This perceived 'cultural minefield' can make people hesitant to be open and transparent until they've worked out the local playing rules.

Can't share because of change

If there is organisational change going on, complete transparency may not be possible. This is natural in times of change, where certain information needs to remain confidential for various reasons, and where answers are yet to be formulated.

The impact of lack of transparency and openness in teams

When transparency is missing, crucial exchange within the team is not happening:

- When team members suspect that someone is hiding something, it makes them cagey and suspicious, which can create gossip and talk behind each other's backs.

- If you don't get the truth in the team, you will look for it elsewhere. This means you spend more time trying to find out the whole story. This is inefficient use of team time, especially if the information was already available somewhere within the team.

- When the truth is not accessible, it's not uncommon for people to fill in the communication gaps with their own hypothesis. This causes assumptions that can be way off track, fuelled by fear and exaggerated speculations. This kind of gossiping is time-consuming and takes the team away from what they are supposed to be doing.

- A team where people gossip and talk behind each other's backs won't be well perceived outside the team. Others can usually pick up on the undertones easily and the team's credibility is negatively affected, as is the credibility and prospects of its individual members.

The impact on the business, customers, employees and stakeholders

There is a growing expectation for organisations to be more and more transparent. There has always been some level of expectancy of openness within organisations, but the transparency that is now being demanded is of a new nature, due to factors such as less hierarchical structures. On top of that, the external world of stakeholders insists on having a greater insight into the inner world of how the company is run. Higher international standards for corporate governance are another influence that feeds more openness. This means everyone's actions and behaviours, particularly leaders', are more closely scrutinised and judged. Everyone is constantly 'on display', 'on stage'. Actions and behaviours are seen and can have consequences. Everyone wants more openness and accessibility to the truth.

Let's look at an example of a company that lacked the practice of transparency.

The company in question has expressed that they value being open and transparent.

Its sales leaders predict the sales results for each quarter. When it then gets to the end of the quarter, there are a lot of surprises as the achieved numbers don't match the predicted ones. The reason for this is that sales leaders have been hiding information and not including it in the prediction, in order to exceed their targets and get better bonuses. So in reality the culture is not that open, and these behaviours make the non-transparency even more inherent.

The impact on the direct reports of the sales leaders is that they feel they have to exceed their predictions. This encourages them to hide information too.

The impact on the sales team is them not being trusted by the rest of the organisation as they appear not to be honest, and working in their own interest.

The potential impact on the customer is one of perceived misalignment of company representatives. If this becomes visible to customers, it could damage the company's reputation. The impact on the organisation is not being able to accurately forecast and shareholders can become uncomfortable that the company is not well led.

The opening story 'George, the angry CEO' is an example of the serious implications that these non-transparent behaviours can have on the bottom line.

A recent news story from the world of business tells us how senior executives have used the corporate jet for travel with their spouses. It might not mean that any rules have been broken but if the actions go against what the company says it stands for and the executives are not forthcoming with information when asked, then the reputation and therefore the value of the organisation can be damaged.

Solutions

Let's face it, transparency is increasingly becoming the expected norm. You know you need to do it. And you know when people do it and when they don't. Transparency, or the lack thereof, is transparent to others.

Like any skill, transparency needs to be practised to become an effective habit.

Let's get specific on how to do it.

Solution 1: Tell the truth

Demonstrate courage by telling the truth. It sounds simplistic, but it's not always easy to be forthcoming with unpleasant truths, as the story of Noel points out. However, by telling the truth, it's not just easier to remember what you've said, it's also demonstrating your integrity.

Think of someone you know who is very open and authentic, who shows who they really are, not just their polished work persona. What positive impact are they having on you? And could you do more to model that and have the same effect?

Solution 2: Reward transparency

When you notice that someone is being transparent and authentic, recognise it, reward it – to encourage others to do the same. You want to reward people because it shows them and others how important transparency is. The reward can be anything from a pat on the back to a more formal reward. By recognising that someone has been transparent, you can create a positive ripple effect where others want to do the same. You are starting to create a culture of openness.

Solution 3: Leaders = role models

Leaders are role models, whether they realise that or not. So if you are the leader, do this quick self-reflection to see where the potential issues are regarding transparency and what you need to focus on.

Which of these reasons are hindering you or your team from being transparent and open:

- Don't dare to tell the truth
- Don't think others can handle or want to hear the truth
- Not being heard by leader
- Don't want to be blamed
- No other outlet
- Not a culture of transparency
- Cultural differences
- Can't share because of change.

Solution 4: Actively reach out to stakeholders

Consider your key stakeholders. Work out who your stakeholders are by plotting them on this mind map.

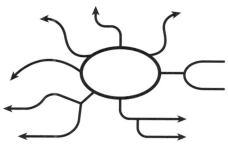

Figure 5.1 Mind map

Then ask yourself: What are they interested in? What do they need you to be transparent about? Whatever it is, this is what you want to be proactive about sharing, because if they have to chase you for that information you will automatically come across as non-transparent at best or as actively hiding something at worst.

For more detail on stakeholder management, go to http://www.leadingteamsbook.com/

Solution 5: Transparently answer a question

In times of change it's not always possible to be transparent, as the answer may not yet be known or not yet possible to communicate. Transparency is then being honest about that. Follow these simple recommendations:

The four principles of answering a question transparently

1. Answer the question.
2. If you don't know the answer, say so.
3. If you cannot answer the questions now, make a commitment for when you will and honour it!
4. If you know the answer but cannot say currently – say so – and make a commitment to share the information when you can.

Solution 6: Have a value of transparency

An organisation has a number of values that make up the culture. Preparing for current and future demands, one of those values should be openness and transparency. You may already have something like it in your company values.

The next step is to clarify what transparency means in your workplace – at an individual, team and organisational level. You need to clarify: What does that mean for us? How does it translate to us?

It could sound something like this:

■ **Individual**: I share my views in a helpful way, even if they are an opposing viewpoint.

■ **Team**: We tell each other what we do and know (our work secrets), so there's no need for secrecy!

■ **Organisational**: We invite other stakeholders to see how we work and operate

Be aware that being open and transparent almost always requires courage, especially if transparency is not yet part of the culture.

Solution 7: Make transparency mandatory

What is measured gets done!

So if you want people to be transparent, put transparency into their goals and objectives. Find the dependency, the link between transparency and results. Help people see how their open and transparent way of working, enables them to achieve more. Effective goals are made up of two parts; WHAT to achieve and HOW to achieve it.

Both WHAT and HOW should contribute equally to performance ratings and therefore pay. Transparency is one of your HOWs and needs to be clearly identified as such in the goal process. Make sure you have goals for the HOW.

Talking behind backs can create a culture of gossip. To avoid this in your team:

1. Review what is being said by asking direct questions to gain clarity. Do not engage with gossip.
2. Provide feedback directly to each other to avoid talking behind each other's backs.
3. Encourage people to say what they want to the person they are talking about – work out 'how to' so it is done in a respectful way.

Let's have a look at what Noel and George could have done instead, had they deployed these solutions.

> Noel knew he had to pluck up courage to talk to George. George wasn't going to be happy about the £500K deficit, but if it went on for longer, the numbers might deteriorate even further.

As he walked into the room, George greeted him with a distracted nod and pointed him to the visitor's chair.

'Hi Noel, how can I help you?'

'I know that you are busy and that you have a lot on with the takeover, but I want to talk to you about something that's very important to me.' Noel slowed down towards the end of the sentence to highlight the seriousness of his request.

He now had George's attention.

'Thank you. I have noticed an error in the predicted sales figure, which means we are currently £500K under budget. I must admit that I hesitated to tell you as you've previously not responded well to bad news.'

George put his pen down and folded his arms.

'Last week at the quarterly review meeting you shouted at Tom when he was being honest with you, so I did think long and hard about coming to see you today. But here I am, because I know you're a good guy and I think you need to know about the deficit. And the sooner we can do something about it the better.' Noel waited for a response.

George was quiet for a bit and then said: 'I'm not happy about this!' angrily tapping his pen on the desk. He then waited a few moments, which seemed like hours to Noel.

Slowly, as the moments passed, George's facial expression changed. He no longer looked as angry as before, in fact he looked tired. George was realising that Noel was trying to help and that he needed to listen to him. He did, and their conversation helped George to see his behaviour pattern and how people felt about giving him bad news. He had had no idea that his reaction was having this effect. So after some more quiet reflection time he decided to be a bit vulnerable by talking to his team, opening up and sharing his feelings of why he reacted that way. He had thought that he was just helping them fix it when he was being aggressive. He thought it was his way of showing power and getting to the results.

> Once he had opened up and they told him what it was really like on the receiving end, it had a huge impact on him, it was a massive eye-opener that had previously completely passed him by.
>
> Opening up to his team also allowed the team to review the issue of the £500 K together and come up with a solution. This meant that the deficit didn't increase further.

Behaviours of team and leader

Under 'Solutions' above, we have listed a number of 'how to' actions. These solutions work best when carried out with these supporting 'how to' behaviours. The actions on their own, will get you only so far. With the right behaviours you can create transparency and openness in the team more effectively.

'How to' solutions	'How to' behaviours	How the behaviours make the difference
Tell the truth.	Show courage	Everyone loves a hero somehow. It's refreshing when someone dares to tell the truth. Having the courage to do so shows strength – you show that you are not afraid to be the voice of honesty.
Reward transparency.	Listen and be observant	Being observant allows you to notice when people are transparent. And when you reward transparency you will get the ripple effect of people doing it more. You will build a culture of greater openness.
Leaders = role models.	Take responsibility	By taking responsibility for your own actions and behaviours, you consider the impact on others and can take control of this impact, not leaving it to chance but staying in as much control as you can to encourage others to follow suit.
Actively reach out to stakeholders.	Be interested	By being interested in your stakeholders you show them that they are important and you build trust which will help you in managing your relationship with your stakeholders and therefore the business.

'How to' solutions	'How to' behaviours	How the behaviours make the difference
Transparently answer a question.	Show courage	Having the courage to say that you don't have the answer is refreshing. Too many people waffle rather than say it straight, and this is never well received. When you show that you have guts, you create trust and people listen to you. More straight-talking is needed.
Have a value of transparency.	Be thoughtful	By carefully considering the value of transparency and how it can support the business, you ensure you understand the links yourself and increase the chance of making others see it too – and being transparent.
Make transparency mandatory.	Be conscientious	By focusing on the 'how' as well as the 'what', people start to behave differently. If you measure it and reward transparency then you will see the difference in team members' behaviours.

Thoughts and feelings of team and leader

On average, a person experiences around 70.000 thoughts per day.[1]

Many of those thoughts are habits that affect a person's mindset or outlook.

What we think affects how we feel, and how we feel affects how we think.

When wanting to create a culture of transparency and openness within a team, actively replace thoughts and feelings that are counterproductive to that. Here are thoughts from the story, their impact on feelings and how they can be changed.

Negative thoughts	Negative feelings	Powerful thoughts	Powerful feelings
I don't know how to break the bad news to George, he has a habit of shooting the messenger and I don't want to get 'shot'.	Nervousness	*His bark is probably worse than his bite. I will go and talk to him and I will get him to listen to me – I know he wants to resolve this too.*	Determination Optimism
He's a bit of a tyrant, isn't he?	Fear	*He's got a temper, but that doesn't make him a bad person.*	Acceptance Understanding
It was becoming increasingly hard to work with George.	Frustration Hesitation	*Who said it's always supposed to be easy! I can learn from this. I am sure he is not aware of the effect he is having on me. Maybe I can help him see that.*	Optimism Tenacity
If my manager is reporting lower numbers than expected then I must do the same.	Uncertainty Anxiety	*I must do what I think is right.*	Courage
There's no point in talking to her, she won't listen anyway.	Helplessness	*I will go and talk to her – it will be different this time. I am sure I can think of a way to make her listen. Let me think about what she wants, that will help me to focus on how I can make her listen.*	Open-minded Curiosity

Summary

Transparency is quickly becoming the expected norm in business and expectations are growing. Increased transparency has great benefits and there are consequences involved with *not* creating a higher level of openness. If you already have a level of openness then strive for more, it will need to increase as we move into the future.

Consequences

There are consequences of not focusing on getting your team to be transparent, there are an increasing number of stories in the press about organisations where the level of openness is not high. The effect can be catastrophic.

Starts at the top

Personal openness starts at the top of any organisation and the more senior you are the more responsibility you have to role model this. Team members watch this and will take on and emulate what the leader or their colleagues do. This is natural, in life we role model what others do; good or bad. However, when done well this can have a very positive cascade effect throughout the organisation.

Reflection questions for the reader

- How open is your team? How much do you and your team demonstrate that you really want to hear open and honest views from others?

- How do you react to people when they are open with you, even if you don't like what they have to say?

- How much responsibility do you take for your actions and their impact on others, when people are open with you?

- How open and transparent are you with other team members? What makes it easy and what stops you?

- How do you reward transparency personally, and as a team?

Self-assessment

After you have implemented the solutions in this chapter, answer these questions again to see the progress you have made.

How would you rate the following in your team?

	1 Very poor	2 Poor	3 Just OK	4 Good	5 Excellent
Transparency and openness					
Trust					
Courage to tell the truth					
Living the values					

6

How do you encourage long-term thinking?

- Increasing the team's ability to focus on the long term
- Increasing the team's awareness of the need to be more strategic and considering the impact of decisions and actions

'The more you chase the Holy Grail of short-term performance, the less you get in long-term results.'

Walter Cabot

Self-assessment

Before reading the chapter, do the following quick self-assessment.

How would you rate the following in your team?

	1 Very poor	2 Poor	3 Just OK	4 Good	5 Excellent
Long-term focus					
Consequence analysis					
Awareness of competition/ marketplace					
Clarity of purpose					

The ever-changing team

Bridget had been going at great speed for a long time and just needed some breathing space. She had asked her assistant to put one hour of thinking time into her calendar. The hour had come and as she rushed into her office, five minutes late for her appointment with herself, she closed the door behind her. A closed door was rare for Bridget, who always wanted to make a point of being accessible.

Bridget was in charge of logistics for a global e-commerce giant. The speed of growth was immense and this meant her division was changing constantly. The kind of changes they saw included a constant stream of new employees as a result of growth as well as high staff turnover. On top of that, the growth meant that people needed to get their head around new processes and business partners at regular

▶

intervals, which also continued to change. This rapid change meant they were only able to see what was in the next month or so. They had seen so many people coming and going that they were almost living week to week. And this was a long-term problem for Bridget and the business. It was causing some self-doubt for Bridget.

There are so many changes that it's only the win of the day that gets the focus. The long-term vision is still valid but people seem to lose track of it. It doesn't seem to matter how many times I talk about it, they are still only dealing with their daily tasks – which I of course want them to do, but we are missing something. I have this inner conflict, I feel frustrated about the lack of future focus, yet I know I have to get the job done. I can feel this inner tension building up. I wonder what it is like for others if this is what it is like for me.

Bridget stood up and walked across the floor to be able to look out the window and get a different perspective.

The conversation I just had with Larry was interesting. He pointed out that people just talk about today and not the future, as they know it's going to change next week anyway, so what's the point?! And something tells me that he's not my only direct report who is experiencing this. I am somehow observing the same thing. I keep trying to get them to lift their heads up and see the bigger picture but I'm not getting the response I want. Maybe I just haven't communicated enough about what it is we are trying to create as an organisation. They need to understand that if we are going to move away from the narrow, blinkered work mode that we are now in, we must operate and behave differently.

We have a lot of eyes on us now. Our growth is attracting investors, which means that we most definitely need to get everything right in the here and now. We cannot afford to have anything other than operational excellence, while we work towards sustaining those results for the future. People just need to understand this and help me make it happen. I am getting frustrated with them.

What else do I have to do?

Bridget looked at her watch. She had only spent 30 minutes of her allotted thinking time, which she had already been late for, and decided that this was all she could afford. There was another crisis looming and as usual, it took priority.

Exploring the problem

In the example above, Bridget is clearly frustrated by the lack of long-term focus in her division. She feels as if she has talked about it extensively but it has not had the desired effect, it has not changed the way people think and operate.

Short-term mentality

The constant change driven by growth drives a short-term mentality where people are just trying to get their daily job done. Balancing the steady flow of new employees with the perpetual process changes, means that any longer-term thinking is stifled, which is even demonstrated by Bridget herself. She's not aware that her own behaviours are counterproductive to what she is trying to achieve, and this is a big part of the problem. Although she is saying that she wants her employees to think about the bigger picture, she is not practising what she preaches. Even her allocated thinking time, where she wanted to take a step back to solve the issue for the future, gets cut short due to another emergency.

Constant change

Larry's message is a diluted version of what his employees are actually experiencing. By the time the information is given to Bridget, Larry has tuned the intensity of the issue down by only conveying the facts and none of the emotions. As employees are expressing that they do not see the point in what they are doing, they are also indicating they are on some level giving up, which is demoralising and can cause people to leave, making the steady flow of new employees even greater. It creates a vicious circle. This also creates constantly changing teams and changing dynamics in those teams.

The reasons for team members having short-term focus

Monthly and quarterly reporting

Short-term reporting of results is necessary in any organisation. However, too much short-term reporting will result in team members concentrating on the short-term results only and not considering longer-term effects of actions.

Difficulty seeing the long-term bigger picture

If team members can't see the big picture (long-term vision/ambition of the company), it's difficult to understand how actions today will drive the future results. It can feel complex and theoretical and hard to grasp, quite literally.

Not enough focus on the marketplace

Not giving time to the strategic business thinking and the impact of the external marketplace and the competition, forces people to just concentrate on the tactical tasks of the day.

Speed of change

When circumstances constantly change, team members may not see the point in looking ahead, as they just expect things to change again.

Emergencies and burning platforms

Many organisations have a culture of 'firefighting', where urgent issues out-trump important ones on a regular basis. Team members will then naturally pay attention to 'whatever/whoever shouts the loudest'. This leads them to focus on putting out the fires in their own area and not to think of the bigger implications. People are just busy and this also becomes part of the culture, where people take pride in being busy and do not want to be seen to 'slow down' and reflect on the bigger picture.

Goals and rewards

If the team is measured on its short-term results, this is naturally what people will go for. What is measured gets done. If team members are not rewarded for thinking long-term, there is no encouragement to change behaviours either.

No clarity of purpose

If the team doesn't understand its purpose, it's hard to see the big picture and see where they fit in, hence hard to consider the impact of what you are doing today and the effect it will have on the future. If you don't have the whole story from all team members, how each role contributes, the tendency will be to focus on your own tasks in isolation.

The impact of short-term focus in teams

With a short-term focus, there's a risk of each member only taking an interest in what they need to get done today. Short-term fire-fighting can create a culture of rushed and reactive work. Then there is potential for errors or even burn-out.

- All decision-making is dependent on the ability to assess outcomes. When long-term focus is missing, it's hard for a team to make decisions as it can't judge the consequences of them. Then important decision-making slows down or doesn't happen at all.

- There is risk of greater conflict due to team members not considering the ramification of what they do on other team members and the team as a whole, as they rush to meet their individual short-term goals.

- There can be frustration as team members may not be able to see what their work leads to, when they are missing the big picture. This can lead to members withdrawing, getting their heads down, being less engaged, hence creating less cooper-ation and not being as effective as they could be. This ulti-mately affects all business results.

The impact of short-term thinking on the business, customers, employees and stakeholders

It's costly to not consider the big picture, the longer term – or have proper planning and thought-through solutions. The costs amass when people work in isolation and/or are unaware of how their individual work has a knock-on effect on colleagues, customers, business partners and other stakeholders.

Short-term thinking is by its nature focused on tasks here and now, so people may be busy with activities but losing the purpose and therefore not taking responsibility for the end results. Everyone is busy but not necessarily on the right things, in the right order and for the right reason. It's rare that people schedule the necessary uninterrupted time to think through plans and actions and what they will lead to.

Let's look at an example.

A call centre used a scorecard where one of the measures was the length of a call. The aim was to keep calls as short as possible in order to be able to take more. This measurement, although well intended, encouraged employees to rush customer calls to get good individual ratings. The consequence of this was unsatisfied customers who had to call back because their issue hadn't been resolved as the employee had not understood the whole issue the first time around. This of course also generated more calls.

The impact was a negative customer experience, which could lead to attrition, as well as a direct cost linked to calls that could and should have been avoided. This example also highlights what happens when employees only look at isolated issues rather than trying to understand the whole picture of the customer's story, or the impact of their own actions.

As this example demonstrates, one of the biggest consequences of short-term, small-picture thinking is how the organisation is perceived by those who experience this mentality and what that perception can lead to.

And if the long-term strategy keeps changing and the organisation doesn't seem to make the links to *why* it is changing then the customer can be affected in yet another way. If the customers don't understand why these changes are happening and the links are not made for them to help them understand, they may become disengaged and ultimately take their business elsewhere.

Here's another example of how short-term thinking dominates a workplace.

A hospital had a target in their accident and emergency department that meant they had a short waiting time as a goal. Hospital staff were very aware that this was sometimes an unrealistic target so they had to use 'work-around' methods to meet this target. At times they moved patients to another area outside of the emergency department just so they could say they achieved the target. In reality that did nothing to solve the long-term issue, it just created a short-term work-around. And it did not help to improve the patient experience or the efficiency of processes.

Solutions

Long-term, big-picture thinking, or taking a holistic view, is not something that just happens automatically. It needs to be given attention. In the example with Bridget, she had the intention to resolve the short-term thinking issues, but she allowed her time to be hijacked by the crises of the day.

Long-term thinking can be encouraged and created.

Let's get specific on how to do it.

Solution 1: Balanced short- and long-term reporting

Put greater focus on *both* short- and long-term reporting of goals and results. They are both important to understand business success and need to run side by side.

Solution 2: Develop people's ability to think long-term

Develop people's understanding of cause and effect, and of what impact actions and behaviours have on stakeholders and results. A quick and simple way to do this is to look at your to do-list and ask yourself what the short and long-term implications (+ or –) of those actions will be. The following Impact Grid gives you a framework to start with.

To do/ action	Short-term impact +/−				Long-term impact +/−			
	People		Planet	Profit	People		Planet	Profit
	Team	Customer			Team	Customer		

Figure 6.1   Impact grid

Solution 3: Study the competition and the marketplace

Share your market intelligence as a team; learn from each other. Read business news. Talk to other people in the business to learn from them. Join external networks. Study your industry. Study your market. Study your competitors.

Ask yourself questions like:

- What is going on out there that I need to know?
- What is going on out there that we need to know about as a team?
- What else do we need to be thinking about that we currently don't know that we don't know?
- How strategic are we versus tactical? Let's take our 'to do' list and ask ourselves: does this fit in the strategic or the tactical? Where should we be spending our time?

Solution 4: Be a 'time owl'

Be wise like an owl about how you spend your time.

Are you focusing on what's important or are you simply responding to what's urgent?

Plan your day, your week, your month and your year(s). Value your own time and that of your team. Schedule regular time for reflection and strategy to make sure your actions are relevant and effective in the long-term. Force yourself to look ahead – and stick to it.

Schedule time for the important priorities, rather than just moving through each day and doing the urgent tasks that appear. By doing this you ensure you lift your head up from the daily tasks and consider the bigger picture.

If you are the team's leader, remember that you set the tone, you are the role model – others will do what you do. So ask yourself: how am I spending my time?

Solution 5: Team goals and rewards

Set both short- and long-term team goals. Short-term goals keep team members focused on what needs to happen now and long-term goals give the bigger picture. When you have both, you start to think more about what you are doing, considering the impact of your actions today into the future. You think: how is what I am doing today going to take me towards that bigger goal? You should be able to see the red thread from what you are doing today right to the future long-term goal, and how it contributes to the organisation's overall vision and purpose.

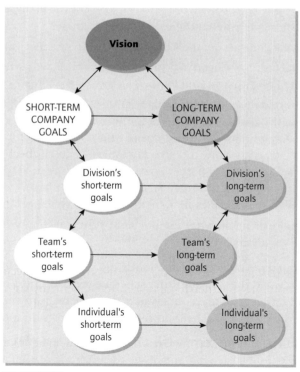

Figure 6.2   The red thread

Linked to the goals, reward and recognise people for long-term thinking. This will encourage the very behaviour you want.

Solution 6: Communicate the overall purpose.

Make absolutely sure that everyone knows the purpose of the team.

- Spend more time together to make the purpose actionable at a team level.
- Make the red thread clear, from each person's role/task to the team's purpose, to the overall purpose/vision of the organisation.
- Sometimes you may need to be explicit about the red thread and the links. You may need to explain and link it to make it understood by others. It is an easy assumption to think that people implicitly understand those links. Make it explicit so there is no ambiguity. This also helps people to see the links for themselves next time.

Solution 7: Invest in team time

Invest in team time, even if the team is changing. When having a fast-changing team (like in Bridget's story), it can be tempting to not take the time to bond as a team, thinking that the team will just change anyway. But unless you do, you're in danger of speeding up turnover even more. It can be as simple as a quick check-in as a team for 15 minutes to align something or you may need to invest the right amount of time for a really big change. In teams, chunky emotional change topics are sometimes given a very short timeslot on the agenda, like 30 minutes. This is better than nothing but you will not gain real buy-in and understanding to the long-term change if topics are shoehorned into a tight agenda. You may think the team has had the discussion but if they haven't connected to it at an emotional level then it is less likely to happen. Any lasting, real transformational change happens at an emotional level.

Solution 8: Take a long-term view on your team members

If you are a leader; no employee is 'yours' forever. People are 'on loan' only and your responsibility is to help them develop, to make more of those resources you've been loaned. Be generous, consider that you have a collective leadership responsibility to think long-term with the resources that you have, even if they won't always be with you. And if all leaders take that collective responsibility then you will reap the rewards through your future employees too.

Solution 9: Make the big picture understandable

Break the big picture into smaller, understandable, actionable pieces, while still keeping the big picture. Show how the smaller pieces fit in. Take one chunk at a time and explain and show the links. Take a step-by-step approach to build a picture from today to the future and show others how you make those connections. Draw a chart, talk about it or tell a story to help make it understandable and get people to make meaning of it.

Stories help people to connect at a powerful, emotional level.

Let's have a look at what Bridget could have done instead, had she deployed these solutions.

Bridget got back to her office just in time for her scheduled strategic hour. She enjoyed these moments of uninterrupted time that she had made into a habit, and for this reason she made sure they were a priority.

There are as always so many changes, that we are in danger of it only being the win of the day that gets the focus. I can see that we are starting to change this though. More and more people are referring to the long-term vision and showing that they are taking responsibility for contributing to it. I know that I have spent much more time thinking about this myself and talking to the teams about it, and it's working, I'm pleased to say. I feel good about the progress we have made.

I remember how Larry used to share how tired his team were of change and how it affected both engagement and people's mood.

We have some good traction going here. We are getting the daily tasks and tactics right. I like the way the team are stopping and making the links to the future. I was asked to attend one of the meetings last week. I watched the team hold a crisis meeting. They put all of their

> ▶ *conflicting priorities onto a flipchart then decided to prioritise them using a chart they have used before but they added a section for long-term impact! I was very happy to see that, so I told them. They seemed thrilled with my comments. I must admit it made me feel better too.*
>
> She spent the rest of her time reflecting on what changes she had seen and also focused on the five-year future plan she was creating. She was remaining honest honest to make sure she didn't fall into the trap of the crisis that kept shouting at her from her desk.
>
> Bridget looked at her watch. Her hour was up. She could have spent more time but knew that there were other things that needed her attention too, so she resolutely got up and headed for a skip-level meeting with her shipping staff. It was time to fill up on intelligence about the current realities of international shipping.

Behaviours of team and leader

Under 'Solutions' above, we have listed a number of 'how to' actions. These solutions work best when carried out with these supporting 'how to' behaviours. The actions on their own will get you only so far. With the right behaviours you can more effectively encourage long-term thinking.

'How to' solutions	'How to' behaviours	How the behaviours make the difference
Balance short- and long-term reporting.	Patience Courage Being different from others and being ok with that	Having patience shows that you are serious about thinking long-term. You are brave enough to wait for results, rather than just going for short-term gratification. People can see that you actually mean what you say when you talk about long-term focus.
Develop people's ability to think long-term.	Show genuine interest	By you showing interest in people's development, you encourage learning. Everyone wants to be seen and heard. Some people are not sure if it is OK to focus on the long-term, and by spending time and developing them, you demonstrate that it matters.

▶

'How to' solutions	'How to' behaviours	How the behaviours make the difference
Study the competition and the marketplace.	Be curious	A natural curiosity in the world around us makes these studies fun to do – and then you make sure you carve out time for them. And it encourages others to do the same.
Be a 'time owl'.	Be rigorous Stop and reflect	Be rigorous and almost force yourself to take the time to look ahead. You reap the rewards and sharing this with the team helps the team too. It also benefits the perception of the team. When other teams see the focus you have on the links to the future they will model that and you will begin to build a culture of long-term thinking.
Team goals and rewards.	Be accountable Be determined	By making the goals realistic with a 50/50 probability of success this motivates team members to want to achieve the stretch targets. Getting rewarded for team goals drives behaviours of support and sharing across the team. As a leader, you show determination about your own goals and keep yourself accountable, and in doing so become a role model. You walk the talk.
Communicate the overall purpose.	Be inspired 'Paint a picture'	If you are inspired about the purpose, others will pick up on that sincerity and be likely to feel the same inspiration. The inspiration and buy-in is also created through the 'picture you paint' of how the purpose feels and what it will lead to.
Invest in team time.	Be rigorous	When you keep your commitment to team time (e.g. team meetings, huddles) you convey the importance of these.
Take a long-term view on your team members.	Be generous	Think of it as karma or whatever you like, but it's true that you reap what you sow. When people recognise your generosity to invest in them (regardless of tenure), they will feel grateful and tend to 'pay back', either through retention or through recommendations, or both.
Make the big picture understandable.	Be inspired Use examples	When you can convey the inspiration you feel about the pieces that make up the big picture, and how they fit in, it becomes more interesting to others and creates a new level of engagement around the work.

Thoughts and feelings of team and leader

On average, a person experiences around 70.000 thoughts per day.[1]

Many of those thoughts are habits that affect a person's mindset or outlook.

> What we think affects how we feel, and how we feel affects how we think.

When wanting to encourage long-term thinking within a team, actively replace thoughts and feelings that are counterproductive to that. Here are thoughts from the story, their impact on feelings and how they can be changed.

Negative thoughts	Negative feelings	Powerful thoughts	Powerful feelings
It doesn't seem to matter how many times I talk about it.	Hopelessness	*I will make sure they hear me, I'll give it another go and do it differently and better this time.*	Determination
Things just keep changing, I can't see the point of thinking long-term – nothing's long-term.	Despair	*I need to make others see the long term. I can make them see it by 'growing up' the idea from today into the future and taking them step-by-step on the journey.*	Resilient
Long term vision is still valid, people seem to lose sight of it	Frustration	*Long term vision is still valid, how can I help people keep sight of it?*	Hope
There are so many changes, it is only the win of the day that gets the focus.	Frustration Hopelessness	*I'm sure people do the best they can. And I think we can focus both short-and long-term if we only start talking about it together.*	Hope Determination
I don't have time to think about this, I need to put out the latest 'fire'.	Stress	*Let's take a moment to reflect. Then I'll be able to put out the fire and make sure it doesn't happen again in the future.*	Control

Summary

Holistic view

It's crucial for businesses and business leaders to be able to take a holistic view, to see the big picture and understand how all parts of the business jigsaw fit together. For a team this means being able to think beyond your own area and recognise how you fit into the wider organisation, and impact the customer experience and the value proposition as a whole. This includes sustainability thinking, which is the ability to contemplate triple bottom lines for long-term business success: People, Planet and Profits (not just the standard bottom line of Profit). The Impact Grid in Solution 2 above includes this thinking.

Taking a long-term view of the business includes being able to assess impact, make decisions and take actions that are not just about an isolated, localised issue.

Busy busy

Everyone is busy, but just being busy is not good enough. If you're not busy with the right things at the right time, you're just wasting time. Long-term success requires long-term thinking, which starts with taking a step back and reflecting on and considering the bigger picture at regular intervals.

Reflection questions for the reader

- Do I spend enough time reflecting on the long-term aspects of my team and our work? Is that enough?
- How much time do I spend on strategy versus tactics?
- Is my team busy being busy? If so, could we, through better long-term thinking, be doing less and achieving more?
- How clear is my team's purpose?
- Does my team have balanced goals?
- How do I encourage people to think long-term?

Self-assessment

After you have implemented the solutions in this chapter, answer these questions again to see the progress you have made.

How would you rate the following in your team?

	1 Very poor	2 Poor	3 Just OK	4 Good	5 Excellent
Long-term focus					
Consequence analysis					
Awareness of competition/ marketplace					
Clarity of purpose					

How do you create a team that delivers and is well perceived?

- Increasing team's awareness of how they are perceived
- Increasing level of responsibility for team delivery and team brand

'I've learned that people will forget what you said, people will forget what you did, but people will never forget how you made them feel.'

Maya Angelou

Self-assessment

Before reading the chapter, do the following quick self-assessment.

How would you rate the following in your team?

	1 Very poor	2 Poor	3 Just OK	4 Good	5 Excellent
Your reputation as a team					
Taking responsibility for your reputation					
Clarity of the team's identity/brand					
Positive behaviours					

Mission impossible

Roger's team was invisible. Everyone knew that they were a system development team, but they kept such a low profile that no one really knew what they were working on until they were nearing an implementation. Then all of a sudden everything was a big rush with communications filled with stress and impossible deadlines.

The latest such communication had landed in the inbox of James, head of finance. He read the request for yet more last-minute, urgent action that was needed for finalising the technical specification. He could feel his face getting hot and red with anger. As this was not the first time he had been given a mission impossible by Roger and his team, he decided that enough is enough and he needed to talk to Roger face to face.

He stomped down the corridor, full of determination. When he got to Roger's office, he knocked and went in without waiting for permission.

Roger was busy as always, but looked up with surprise as James entered.

'Hi James. I'm in the middle of something here, how can I help you?'

James' ensuing monologue left nothing unsaid. He expressed his frustration with the constant last-minute requests that were impossible to meet. He questioned the way Roger's team was working when everything seemed to be a fire drill.

Roger listened carefully and tried not to get defensive, but inside he felt like his leadership was being attacked. It was not a good feeling.

'Well, I don't know. I've been so busy. I need to check with my team. I'll get back to you.'

James curtly nodded, spun around and left the room. 'Yes, do that.'

Roger called his team together straightaway and explained that Finance was infuriated with the request they had received.

The team members started talking over each other, recognising that the timeframes were tight but having been so busy as always, they didn't think they could have done anything differently. The team continued to blame another team and an external partner for not having provided them with critical information on time. His team was basically saying that it was not their fault. At some point in the conversation they started pointing a finger at Roger too, surprised at his outburst, wondering why he hadn't spoken up earlier if this was seen as a reoccurring problem.

Reluctantly he had to take on their point. He was embarrassed. He should have taken control sooner.

Later that day, Roger got a phone call from Felicity, the marketing manager who was now a trusted peer.

'Hey Roger. I need to talk to you. I'll get straight to the point. I think your team's and therefore your reputation is being damaged by this latest project you're working on. There's a lot of noise around how you are handling this and a sense of blaming that's not doing you any favours.'

Roger sighed. This day was not getting any better.

Exploring the problem

Roger's team is not doing a good job at communicating progress regularly. They only communicate when they *really* need something, which then appears urgent to others who weren't kept in the loop of how things were going.

Reputation

Late requests for input create stress and irritation in those who feel they've been given a mission impossible. This irritation makes them less willing to co-operate. And now, Roger's team is starting to get a reputation as a team who doesn't know what they are doing. The team, as well as the individuals in the team, potentially now have their credibility questioned.

The last-minute approach has been building over time, and has therefore come to a head for James. He loses his temper with Roger. When anger is involved, rationality is no longer present and constructive outcomes are hard to get to.

Blame

Roger feels attacked and defensive, even if he's trying not to show that. He turns some of his frustration, the mild form of anger, on his team who start blaming others rather than taking responsibility for their impact.

As this shows, a team that is not delivering as expected will also not be well perceived. And a team that is not well perceived, gets a bad reputation. And from a bad reputation, it's hard to get the trust and co-operation from others, which they need to be able to do their job well.

The reasons for teams not delivering and not being well perceived

They are not able to do their job

If team members are lacking the skills or the tools to do their job, it is difficult for them to deliver as expected. This can also be a reflection of them not being *able* to do the job to the best of their ability, if it's too scripted, not making the best use of each person's specific strengths and capabilities.

They don't work well together

A team that lacks in trust and/or teamwork will find it hard to do their jobs as effectively as they could, working side by side but not necessarily together.

They don't know what's expected of them

Without clear roles and responsibilities, goals and expectations, team members do very little *or* they do what they individually decide could be expected of them. They may even make team assumptions of what they are expected to do, which could take them off track.

They miss deadlines

Delivering to expectations and plans is crucial for trust. If a team keeps missing deadlines for any of the reasons listed here, their reputation will be impacted.

They make excuses and are not prepared

Excuses are never fun to listen to. When team members are not prepared, they often fall back on making excuses as to why something hasn't been done or done properly.

They are not correctly estimating what the job involves

When team members are quick to jump to action, they may not have taken the time to assess what it will take to complete the task. They end up overwhelmed and unable to deliver while the clock is ticking.

They demonstrate negative behaviour

Team members who blame others and circumstances for not delivering as expected, erode the trust others could have in them. This is also true when others can observe ongoing conflict in the team, when team members talk behind each other's backs, and it is not dealt with or resolved by the leader or team members.

They don't tell people what they are doing

Teams that keep to themselves or don't think about the importance of managing their stakeholders, or communicating regularly, can find themselves without the support they need to be able to perform.

The impact of not delivering and not being well perceived in teams

- When a team is not delivering, others don't want to work with them or be dependent on them. Not delivering makes the team poorly perceived. It creates a lack of trust and the team gets a bad reputation.
- It's harder for the team to do their work when collaboration is withheld.
- It's harder to recruit into the team when there is reluctance to join.

The impact on the business, customers, employees and stakeholders

When a promise of delivery is not met, relationships are negatively affected. People feel let down and disappointed. It leads to a lack of trust.

Teams with a bad reputation, who aren't delivering, will make it hard for other teams to do their job, impacting the collaboration across the business. Even if asking for help, such a team may not get the help they need, further impacting the business delivery. People will not go out of their way to help them.

Employees' behaviours and lack of delivery can be experienced both on the inside and from the outside of the business. When a customer is directly affected and don't get what they've paid for, they may choose to take their business elsewhere.

It can affect the organisation's brand overall and therefore its perceived value. A tarnished brand has a harder time attracting investors, customers and top employees. Not managing reputation and brand carefully can be very expensive.

If people feel too scripted or restricted in *how* to carry out their job, delivery is likely to be negatively impacted, as is employee engagement.

A team who were part of a large multinational organisation was known for constantly being busy and putting out fires. They moved from fire drill to fire drill. They jumped from action to action and simply reacted to requests. Their results were unpredictable and other teams were unsure of them so they avoided doing any work with them unless they absolutely had to.

The team was seen as always reacting and responding rather than being proactive. It was hard to work with them. This 'fire drill' behaviour stopped them from taking time out to plan ahead and get out of this reactive state. Others were not confident in their delivery so the reputation of the team was not positive and word got around the organisation quickly.

The impact was even worse, as the leader of the team then got fired and this set back the team even further. It also cost a lot of time and money to rebuild the team along with its reputation and trustworthiness.

Solutions

It's human nature to want to have some level of autonomy. When wanting a team to deliver well, this is one of the strategies worth considering. Think about giving your team members as much freedom as possible to do their job in the way they want to do it, making it possible for them to deliver at the top of their ability.

Ultimately it's about creating various opportunities for teams to be able to perform well and create a good, solid impression.

Let's get specific on how to do it.

Solution 1: Performance management

Getting a team to perform is one of the biggest responsibilities of a leader. It comes down to setting goals with the team members, in line with the vision of the organisation.

> Great goals put equal importance on WHAT and HOW. The performance management system must have a rating for achievement of goals *as well as* a behaviour rating.

And once these goals are set, creating plans as to how the goals will be achieved, what to do to get there. This also involves equipping the members to achieve the goals, identifying strengths to use and areas to develop. Then follows regular coaching and follow-up, to ensure the person can perform to plan. It's a continuous loop.

Figure 7.1 Performance management

Solution 2: Success habit creation

Creating a success habit can work well for a team who needs to focus on turning something from a negative into a positive. It is commonly agreed that it takes at least 21 days to make a habit and 21 days to break a habit. By creating a habit of success it means you are focusing your time and energy on something you want, NOT something you don't want. For example, if you want to create a habit of meeting deadlines you need to put an emphasis on it and build a plan to make it work. There will be members of a team who are driven to hit deadlines and will work very well at achieving them, so use the person(s) in the team with that skill and use their methodology to help the other members of the team to build a success habit for meeting deadlines.

Review the success habits in your team and build habits for the whole team to follow. Use accountability buddies to hold each other to account on your success habit plans.

Solution 3: Take responsibility

Take responsibility for the team's reputation. Use the 'moment of truth' to think about your responses. This is the moment where we make a choice. That choice determines the results we get at any given time. This applies to you personally or to you as a member of a team. As the diagram below illustrates, the moment between the stimulus – when someone makes a comment – and the response you make – is the 'moment of truth'. This is where you choose how to respond. It is only a moment, a second or even a blink of an eye, but this is the opportunity you have to *choose* to respond in a way that affects the impact you have in a constructive way. Responses don't have to be automatic, but due to our habits of thought, they often are, unless we take control.

As a team, choose that 'moment of truth', rather than being run by your 'team autopilot', to ensure you are improving the perception of the team. Every moment counts.

Figure 7.2   **Moment of truth**

Take responsibility also for the decisions that you make as a team. If you've made a decision, you need to stand by that decision as a team, backing each other up, not going off and doing something other than what was agreed.

Solution 4: Reframing learnings into better solutions

Teams can learn something new every day. There is great power in taking learning from a situation and turning it into a better solution. This is called reframing, simply seeing all results as learning. Each team member can reframe outcomes and results. Reframing is also an excellent way of being seen as delivering, it helps other people to experience the positive way forward. A team who builds a culture of reframing can do so simply by seeing things differently and communicating that each stage is a learning to take you to something better, even greater.

Start reframing in your team and take on board all the learning. Hold a learning set, and focus on talking about what you need to reframe or learn from.

There was a team who were breaking new ground in the work they were carrying out. Everything they did was new and no one else had previously done it. They were not attached to the activities they were implementing or carrying out. They simply kept trying new things to create greater results. The reputation they had was that they were very successful and everything they did was seen as a positive step forward. People even quoted them as a team that pretty much got it right all the time. They were highly respected.

They didn't get it right each time though. It was just the way they reframed it when it didn't go the right way, which made it look that way. The team knew they had to break new ground and to do that they would have to make some errors along the way. They saw those errors as learning opportunities and the learning helped them to get it right. They were both positive and realistic, which made people feel connected to them and what they were trying to achieve. This translated into them being seen as highly successful. And they were, but only because they dared to try things and not get beaten down by setbacks on the way.

Solution 5: Ask for feedback to understand perception

Go and find out what the perception of the team is. Ask people what they think of your team, ask them for feedback. Use this simple four-step method:

1. Decide as a team who you want to get feedback from, in order to gain an understanding of how your team is perceived.

2. Ask for feedback: you want to know about your team's strengths as well as areas where you could do more to add value. Ask people how your team makes them feel and what impact you have as a team. (In order to ellicit open and honest observations, it is a good idea to get someone who is not in the team to ask the questions.)

3. Discuss the responses you get as a team. Find solutions to maximise your team's strengths and to improve the development areas identified, in order to create the reputation you want. Work on the behaviours you need to demonstrate as a team to support these actions.

4. Communicate back to those who gave you feedback. Tell them what you are doing with their feedback and how you are using it.

Figure 7.3 **Feedback for the team**

Solution 6: Manage your reputation

How a team is perceived creates their reputation, which needs to be managed rather than left to chance. Each team has an image whether they manage it or not, so take control of that image and reputation. Consider your stakeholders, what they expect, what you deliver and hence what your reputation becomes. And if you have already implemented solution 5, you will have plenty to kick-start the discussion with.

Ask your team these questions:

■ How is our team perceived?

■ If we were to ask others about our team what would they say? Would it be positive and constructive? Do we know this already?

■ What behaviours do the team demonstrate that are useful and not useful? What is the impact on others?

■ How would you describe the relationship between this team and its customers, both internal and external?

Solution 7: Build your team's brand

A brand is a concept, an expectation, which lives in the head of the customer.

In general, you could say that the brand is made up of the product itself, the service that surrounds it and the communication that's used about it. When all these things are added together, an experience is created, a promise of what the customer can expect, which can be called a brand promise. And a team has both brand and brand promise.

As a team, think about why it is important to work on the brand the team has. To be successful it is very important to be a reliable partner for your internal and external stakeholders, to deliver a good experience. So, if you're not doing it already, think of others in the organisation as the customer. This thinking changes the mindset, it puts you into a different frame of thinking. Would you treat external customers the way you do internal colleagues? What if you treated internal colleagues like customers? And what if you treated your employees like customers?

Here are some discussion questions for your team:

- How clear is our team identity/brand?
- How much do people know about what we do? How are we communicating about our 'brand promise' and delivery?
- How could we raise the profile of our team?
- In what way would it change the perception of our team if we treated our internal colleagues like customers?

Let's have a look at what Roger could have done instead, had he deployed these solutions.

> Roger had thought a lot about his team and how they were being perceived by others. He had discussed the subject with his team in depth, and they had all agreed that it was crucial to their success to become more proactive in their way of working. One of his team members had been given the overall responsibility of communication.

▶ This meant they now had a communication plan, which carefully tracked all relevant stakeholders and how they needed to be involved and communicated with, through the complete cycle of a project and its implementation.

And the results were very encouraging. The ease of the latest implementation had been praised by a number of people around the organisation. The feedback he was particularly pleased with was the pat on the back he had received from James in Finance, who was known for his structured approach, rarely matched by others.

All our lives are so much easier these days, I actually feel in control and so much calmer.

It makes me wish I had taken this proactive approach to my team earlier, but better late than never!

Behaviours of team and leader

Under 'Solutions' above, we have listed a number of 'how to' actions. These solutions work best when carried out with these supporting 'how to' behaviours. The actions on their own will get you only so far. With the right behaviours you can create a team that delivers more effectively and is well perceived.

'How to' solutions	'How to' behaviours	How the behaviours make the difference
Get the best out of your team with performance management.	Be interested Be inspired	With genuine interest and inspiration, you can make others interested and inspired to perform. When you show your belief in them and make it possible to be successful, you light a fire that propels performance.
Create a success habit.	Be determined Be responsible	By taking responsibility for the creation of the success habit, you feel like you are taking action towards something you want. This drives you on to do it again. The repetition and the success you create drives you to take the next step.

▶

'How to' solutions	'How to' behaviours	How the behaviours make the difference
Take responsibility.	Be brave	By taking responsibility you are taking control of the outcome you would like to have. You are choosing the impact that you have which has a lasting effect on your reputation, beyond any action you may take. You show strength and determination by being brave.
Reframe learnings into better solutions.	Be positive Show a 'can do' attitude	By having this 'can do' attitude and seeing everything as a learning, you are seen as a team who creates great things, even through tough times. You create a culture of learning. In the words of life coach Anthony Robbins: 'There is no such thing as failure only results!'
Ask for feedback to understand perception.	Be inspiring Be brave	In the long run, it is not what you say, it is how you make people feel, that matters. This affects the perception you create, whether in the team or for you personally. By being brave and open to that feedback, you are inspiring to others. You not only get feedback but the way you are perceived has an immediate boost too.
Manage your reputation.	Be proud	Be proud of your team and make it your mission to manage the team reputation. This gives others a sense of pride too. By being attached and associated with the team's brand people want to be part of creating something positive which gives them a sense of worth.
Build your team's brand.	Be caring	By showing your stakeholders that you care enough about them to consider your brand (as your brand is all about the value you give to them), you build a relevant brand that's about more than just the team.

Thoughts and feelings of team and leader

On average, a person experiences around 70.000 thoughts per day.[1]

Many of those thoughts are habits that affect a person's mindset or outlook.

What we think affects how we feel, and how we feel affects how we think.

When wanting to ensure that a team delivers and is well perceived, actively replace thoughts and feelings that are counterproductive to that. Here are thoughts from the story, their impact on feelings and how they can be changed.

Negative thoughts	Negative feelings	Powerful thoughts	Powerful feelings
I've been given another mission impossible, enough is enough!	Irritation Animosity	*I like challenges. What can I do with what I have been given now?*	Curious Hope
I question the way Roger's team is working. Everything is a fire drill with them!	Aggressive	*I am inquisitive and want to understand more about Roger's team and the way they work.*	Interested
My leadership is being attacked. This is not a good feeling.	Discouraged	*I am going to keep an open mind and listen carefully to learn. I feel OK with this.*	Satisfied
It's not my fault, it's them.	Resentful	*I can take responsibility for this. I can review what I am doing to support this.*	Receptive
I'm embarrassed. I should have taken control earlier.	Disappointed	*I can take control now and make this right from this point onwards.*	Confident
This day is not getting any better.	Anxious	*It's all happening perfectly and it will get better.*	Fascinated

Summary

Every team has a team brand, an image and a reputation, created by the actions and behaviours of the team and its individuals. And a large part of that perception is driven by how well the team delivers on expectations and promises made.

As a team you need to make sure that everyone understands and takes responsibility for their role in creating the perception of the team, which includes both what is delivered and how it is delivered (e.g. on time, respectfully and professionally).

As a leader of a team, you need to create the environment and infrastructure that allows for the team to deliver to expectation.

> 'A leader is not necessarily the one who does the greatest things, it is the one that gets the people to do the greatest things.'
> Ronald Reagan

Reflection questions for the reader

- How much responsibility am I taking for my own and my team's reputation?
- How well does my team deliver to deadlines?
- To what degree do I make excuses when I or my team don't deliver as expected?
- How much am I proactively creating success habits to ensure delivery?

Self-assessment

After you have implemented the solutions in this chapter, answer these questions again to see the progress you have made.

How would you rate the following in your team?

	1 Very poor	2 Poor	3 Just OK	4 Good	5 Excellent
Your reputation as a team					
Taking responsibility for your reputation					
Clarity of the team's identity/brand					

8

How do you get a team to manage change effectively?

- Increasing effectiveness of change management in teams
- Minimising disruption during times of change

'Whosoever desires constant success must change his conduct with the times.'

Niccolo Machiavelli

Self-assessment

Before reading the chapter, do the following quick self-assessment.

How would you rate the following in your team?

	1	2	3	4	5
	Very poor	Poor	Just OK	Good	Excellent
Effectiveness of change implementation					
Acceptance of change					
Dealing with change					
Proactively leading change					

Have you seen the email?

Jenna was at her desk, struggling to get her work finished to close off the week. It was 4 pm and the familiar pinging sound of a new email broke through her concentration. Part of her didn't want to look at it for fear of getting distracted, but as she had seen that it was from one of the executives who rarely communicated directly with people, the temptation was too great. The email title read: *New Performance Criteria*. She just had to open it.

As Jenna got into the details of the email, she experienced a sinking feeling in her stomach. *What is this?! And what does this mean for me?!*

The email was explaining the arrival of a new way of assessing and rewarding performance. Up until then they had only been rated on *what* they were doing, i.e. achieving their goals. As of 1 January they

▶

would now also be judged on *how* they achieved their goals. In fact, 50 per cent of their performance rating would now be dependent on their behaviours.

The behaviour rating would factor in feedback from employees' manager, colleagues, direct reports and in some cases even customers. This change meant that the performance rating would put new expectations on employees, and would also affect pay and potential bonus. The reason for the change was quoted as wanting to create a more comprehensive assessment, which would also encourage behaviours in line with the corporate values.

I can't believe they are springing the news on us like this! They can't be serious! This could affect me badly, it could impact my pay and maybe I wouldn't be able to send the kids on the school trip to Italy. And that holiday we have booked! How are they thinking this is going to work? What if people are not fair but vindictive? Will I be punished just because I didn't see eye to eye with one of my colleagues and they decide to mark me down? This is crazy!

Jenna glanced at her watch, conscious of time, but still decided to call her office confidant, Peter.

'Have you seen the email?!' Was the first thing she said as he answered her call.

'I did! I was just about to call you. I have bad feelings about this. I think this will be used as a loophole to get rid of certain people. If you're not one of their favourites, you will get a bad review, regardless of how hard you've worked.'

'Am I right in thinking that if I don't get a good behaviour rating, my overall rating is impacted and I may not get the expected raises or even a smaller bonus?'

'Well, that's how I read it, but it's not clear exactly how it will work.' Peter retorted.

After the weekend, Jenna and Peter picked up where they had left off. The speculations continued well into the morning without them becoming any the wiser, only more stressed.

Exploring the problem

Jenna is taken by surprise to have such a major change communicated in a simple, short email.

Rational and logical

The email is rational and logical in its presentation, but does nothing to consider the impact on the receiver and how it will make them feel. The communication method was not the best choice for a message raising both questions and concerns, none of which could be satisfied by reading the email.

The shock of the message makes her worry straight away about her own personal circumstances. Jenna has an emotional reaction where she is not able to look at the information calmly and objectively.

Emotions

The fear she experiences, makes Jenna go into a defensive, protective mode. She goes straight from a work-related situation to her personal life and the worry of how that will be affected.

Feeling defensive and protective, makes Jenna want to have this feeling validated and so she turns to Peter for that. As they are now colluding with each other rather than communicating directly with the source, they are having a negative impact on the productivity of the team. They are talking about what has happened rather than getting on with the job. This is natural human behaviour when we don't fully understand why or how the change will affect us.

Involvement

When changes happen without any employee involvement or consultation, resistance is a common response. It makes people feel unimportant and overlooked and they may say things like: 'Why didn't they ask us?' or 'We could have told them ...'.

Another problem with change is that it always creates a sense of loss, as you're leaving something behind that was very familiar to you, or something you knew you could handle, and moving onto something new and less known. And if it feels like no one is listening or understanding, the feeling lingers.

The reasons for teams not managing change effectively

Fear of the new or unknown

If people don't know how they will be impacted by a change or how they will be able to handle it, it's natural to experience a feeling of fear.

Too much change, too fast

When several changes come in rapid succession, without the team having had a chance to get their head around the previous ones, it becomes overwhelming and creates inertia. Team members don't deal properly with the change as it seems pointless.

Teams don't understand the dynamics of change

The team members have not been made aware of the predictable stages of change that people go through every time a new change happens. As a result, they don't recognise that they are having a natural reaction nor know how to best manage the stage they are in.

People get stuck in denial

Denial is the first natural stage of the change curve. By acting as if the change can't possibly be happening (denial, resistance), there is no acceptance of change and therefore no drive to manage it either.

The leader is at a different stage of the change curve

Most of the time, leaders are aware of upcoming changes ahead of their teams. They may have had a fair amount of time to think about the change and prepare for it themselves, as a leader, before they communicate it. They are then in danger of communicating it from a standpoint of someone who's further along on the change curve than the person receiving the message. (For more on the change curve, see under 'Solutions' below).

If this is the case, the leader is not demonstrating that he/she understands the impact of change on the team, and is not communicating on the same wavelength.

People don't agree with the change or understand it

If team members don't know why a change is happening or how it's going to work, they will feel frustrated. If they don't agree with the change, they may start to fight it. Either way, the change progression is slowed down.

People feel like change is forced on them

When team members are not involved or have not been consulted in the change decision, but are served a *fait accompli*, it can feel as if the changed is forced on them. They don't feel a part of the change, so they resist it or actively work against it.

There is too much negativity around the change

Pessimism breeds pessimism. If someone is surrounded by negativity, they would have to consciously think differently to not feel negative themselves.

The impact of not managing change effectively in teams

When change is not carefully managed, the team can be dramatically affected. The introduction of change is often perceived as sudden, even if the communicator has thought about it for some time. The reactions to the suddenness can make things fraught in the team.

- It creates stress, which affects the mood, hence conflict and unnecessary strain on relationships across the team occur.
- When team members feel unsure and spend time speculating about the change, it takes their focus away from their work. Energy and engagement levels drop.
- If a change is not properly thought-through and planned, change implementation will be less effective and the team less productive.

The impact on the business, customers, employees and stakeholders

These impacts on the team lead to a drop in productivity, which is always costly.

Uncertainty and stress can cause friction and conflict with other departments too, which affects morale and productivity beyond the team.

The example below also highlights the issue of a leader who is further along on the change curve and who has not consulted anyone in the process.

The new leader had thought about the reorganisation and the changes he was going to make for three months. Plenty of time for him to get used to the idea. He was under time pressure to turn around results within the next six months so he knew speed and efficiency were of the essence. He sent an email to all his employees announcing a new organisation structure that would come into play in one month's time.

His email was met with silence and he was pleased to see that everyone was happy with the change. This was of course not the case, but he had incorrectly interpreted silence as acceptance. He didn't realise this until his boss angrily approached him asking him about the commotion that had broken out in the office. Speculation and defensive behaviours had taken grip of the workforce as a result of his poor change communication and not having considering the impact on others. One conversation he had overheard on the floor went something like this:

'I feel run over, unimportant – like I'm an outsider who's not important enough for my manager to spend time on. It feels so impersonal, as if we are dispensable and should just obey orders. My trust is gone and I don't know what's going on.'

Employee stress and low morale can lead to wasteful absenteeism and turnover.

Customer experience can be negatively impacted through worried/ stressed employees as well as ineffective, changing processes that are badly managed. This can damage image and reputation.

Solutions

Effective change management does not happen by chance. You need to have a planned, thought-through approach to make people want to embrace the change and come along with you. This we call 'Change Leadership'. To help team members deal with change, you need to help them focus on what they can influence or control rather than worry about what they can't.

The change curve

The change curve exists in a number of different versions. What they all have in common is that there are four predictable stages that people always go through in times of change. If carefully managed, the time it takes to go through each stage can be reduced.

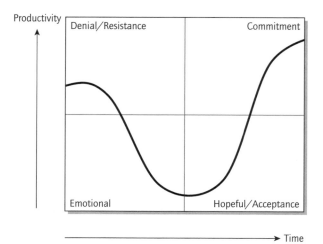

Figure 8.1   The change curve

See Solution 4 below, for details of the change curve.

People typically change their behaviours out of pleasure or pain. It's either too painful to keep doing what you're doing or it will be so rewarding to change that you do it for that reason.

To manage change effectively in teams, you continuously have to think about your team members; where they are on the change curve, how they feel, and how to approach them in a way that matches their needs, so that necessary change can happen at a faster pace.

Think about how you can communicate to help people see the possibilities of change. Help people understand that they can cope with it. Give them coping strategies by using these solutions. Let's get specific on how to do it.

Solution 1: Strategy and communication plan

Create a detailed strategy and communication plan for your change, clarifying what you will achieve, how you will achieve it and how you will communicate throughout the change.

Careful planning forces you to think through the various steps of the change, and how to approach the people involved and overcome obstacles.

Following through on the strategy and plan creates a checking mechanism, which keeps you on track and allows you to gauge how you're doing and measure the success of the change. Here are some ideas for contents to get you started.

CHANGE GOAL – What we will achieve and why it's so important								
Change implementation plan				Change communication plan				
What to do	Who will do it	When to do it	Measure of success	What to communicate	Who will do it	To whom	Where: channel	When

Figure 8.2 Change strategy and communication plan

Solution 2: Slow down

The speed the leader is operating at in the change is often perceived as too fast. If the leader is far ahead of the rest of the team then he/she needs to slow down. Slow down and check that people are all at the same point. Stop and reflect to make sure you are prioritising changes, doing the right thing at the right time – and doing it right. Getting it right first time is better than having to re-do the change. Quality over quantity is important to increase belief in the change.

Solution 3: Positive reinforcements of strengths

When change occurs people can get into focusing on what is wrong, rather than what is right, and this can start to get personal as people try to push the blame onto others. Using strengths is a powerful method to help yourself and others through change.

Try this simple exercise:

Interview each other on strengths: *Tell me, when did you see me at my best? When, where and what?* Then write down your top four or five strengths in only a word or two. This helps to remind yourselves of your strengths and where and how you can use them in times of change. It can also help you to remain positive during change.

Solution 4: Communicate the change curve

Help people understand the predictable stages you always go through in times of change. Give them solutions for how to manage the four stages of the change curve.

Phase 1: The denial/resistance phase

When people are in the denial phase you need to communicate but don't give them too much at this point. Give them enough information, so that they understand that the change is happening, but don't overwhelm them with too much too soon. They need communication little and often. Make sure people know where to go for answers. Make sure you are available to answer questions to help them move through the change curve into the next phase.

Phase 2: The emotional phase

During this phase fear, anger, resentment and uncertainty start to come into play. Team members may need to vent their anger and share how they feel. In carefully planning this phase, you need to have thought through the obstacles and objections people will bring up. Also really think about the impact the change has. Be ready to listen and allow people to talk about what they are experiencing. If this is not managed effectively it can send you into chaos. People who don't feel like anyone understands what they are feeling tend to stay in the emotional phase. Be prepared to listen and help people to get answers to their concerns, so that they can move on to the next phase.

Phase 3: The hopeful/acceptance phase

The team members are now moving towards the change and are ready to explore more in terms of what it means for them. They are also considering how they can start to make it work and can start to contribute with ideas for the change implementation. Be ready with any training and support here. Also give them experiences of what the change will bring and what it will be like. Talk about and show them what it will be like in the change.

Phase 4: Commitment

The team members have come through the change and accepted it and it is now happening. Don't forget at this point to celebrate success and the achievements that have been made along the way. This will reinforce the positives of the change and make it easier next time you want to implement change.

Solution 5: Recognising that you are not at the same stage as others

As a leader, you are always a step ahead, sometimes several steps ahead, of change depending on your seniority and role. You could have been talking, thinking about and exploring the change for a while. You could be in the commitment phase and the rest of the team could still be in the denial/resistance phase. So you have to go back and communicate to the team from where *they* are on the change curve, not where you are. Remember to show empathy, remember what it was like to be at that stage.

Solution 6: Demonstrating emotional intelligence

When you address others who are going through change, you need to put yourself in their shoes. Doing that forces you to think of the change from their perspective. As a result, you are much more likely to communicate with them in a place where they will hear you and come along with you. Be emotionally aware of the impact of the change. Have your radar on so you can be aware of the effect of what you are doing and saying. Your behaviours are speaking louder than you are.

Solution 7: Communicate, communicate, communicate

Communication when dealing with change means two-way communication, all the way through the various stages of the change curve. Listening and involving people, and letting them share their thoughts and concerns, are critical along the path. People are often too busy pushing ahead with the change, preoccupied with creating fast change, but leaving the rest of the team behind; they may end up having to work through the whole change process again. The law of communication applies here. You need loads of it. You need to communicate seven times in seven different ways to reach everyone, so get creative with your communication around change.

Solution 8: Know that people are convinced in different ways

When decision-making impacts change, be aware that people will be convinced in different ways. Some will want the facts, in which case you will need to use a logical approach and a rational, analytical style to convince them. Others will want to understand how the change will impact them personally, in which case you will need to show that you have considered this. How people feel impacts the behaviours in the team and how connected and engaged they will be with the change. They will also want to understand how that is portrayed to others. Everyone will want to know the reasons for change and the context for the change. Ensure you make the links and connections using both styles.

Solution 9: Team decision-making

Allow the team to get involved in decisions in times of change. Call meetings, allow people to discuss the challenges, obstacles and the positive aspects of the change. Help them focus on the possible solutions and benefits. This may feel like it is taking more time than necessary, but if you haven't got people on board you will have to go back and rework it all again so this investment of time upfront will actually save you time. Allow team members to understand the change by being a part of the solution.

Let's have a look at what Jenna's company could have done instead, had they deployed these solutions.

The senior leaders had discussed a revised performance assessment system for some time and it was now time to let the employees know about it too. Before the meeting they reflected on how they should communicate. They carefully planned the meeting, remembering that the people in the room would be in a different stage of the change curve to them and they needed to take this into account. It was going to be an interactive meeting with lots of room for questions and time to create understanding.

Jenna was invited to an information meeting with her manager, together with her peers, who were all in people leadership positions. She was curious, as an updated performance assessment system had been discussed for the last few months. She had been invited to give input on it, both as someone who held performance reviews with her direct reports and as an individual performer.

When they were all seated, her manager kicked it off by saying:

'Thanks for coming. As you know we're here to look at the new, *highly awaited* performance management approach.' He smiled as he stressed the words 'highly awaited'.

'Here it is.' He gestured to a slide that showed an overview of the assessment criteria.

'As you know, we have wanted to create a fairer and more complete assessment. Previously, we were only assessing goal achievement, regardless of how people got there. We will now also be assessing how the goal was achieved, how someone behaved and interacted with others to get the job done. We believe, as I think you do too, that this will help encourage greater teamwork and better communication as well as better goal achievement. Let me go through the details and then we can discuss any questions you may have. Does that sound OK?'

Jenna found herself nodding. She was sure there would be some question marks but overall it was looking OK. As she had been involved in the exploring process, she also knew that her initial concerns had been taken care of. And she felt sure that any outstanding concerns would be taken seriously too and hopefully resolved.

Behaviours of team and leader

Under 'Solutions' above, we have listed a number of 'how to' actions. These solutions work best when carried out with these supporting 'how to' behaviours. The actions on their own will get you only so far. With the right behaviours you can get your team to manage change effectively more effectively.

'How to' solutions	'How to' behaviours	How the behaviours make the difference
Create a strategy and communication plan.	Being proactive	Actively seeking a solution to the change and detailing a plan helps you to cover all aspects and it makes you proactively review how you are communicating.
Slow down.	Being reflective	Just stopping and taking a moment to reflect on where you are is as important as being proactive. When we stop, take time out and think about the change and how we are behaving through change, it helps us to put things into perspective and see our actions more clearly and the impact they have on others as well as the change.

'How to' solutions	'How to' behaviours	How the behaviours make the difference
Positively reinforce strengths.	Being positive Being considerate	By focusing on the strengths of others when we are dealing with change we move into a positive mindset. It forces us to embed the strengths for the other person and display that good intention to help others.
Communicate the change curve.	Being trustworthy Being conscientious	These are predictable stages of change, so being trusted and conscientious in how you handle the changes supports people. Actively and explicitly talking about the stages of change makes the change happen quicker. You simply want to help them through the change curve as quickly as you can.
Recognise that you are not at the same stage as others.	Demonstrating empathy	Meeting people where they are in response to a certain change, rather than where you are creates quicker buy-in. It moves them through the change towards commitment at a faster pace.
Demonstrate emotional intelligence.	Being sensitive Being responsible	Being aware of your behaviours and the impact you have in change means you will be focusing on the WHAT of the change as well as the HOW. Transformational change happens at a behavioural level.
Communicate, communicate, communicate.	Being creative Being brave	Getting creative about communication, and thinking differently about how you do it, motivates people to create the change with you so they own it and feel connected to it. Then they make it happen.
Know that people are convinced in different ways.	Being courageous Being open minded	By using different styles to influence team members in change, you are matching their needs and helping them to understand in a way that connects with them. Change happens at a quicker pace.
Involve the team in decision-making.	Being adaptable Being cooperative	Cooperating and allowing team members to make team decisions brings clarity and allows people to confront the emotional aspects of the change. This supports them in coming to terms with it and moving on to make the change happen.

Thoughts and feelings of team and leader

On average, a person experiences around 70.000 thoughts per day.[1]

Many of those thoughts are habits that affect a person's mindset or outlook.

What we think affects how we feel, and how we feel affects how we think.

When wanting to manage change effectively, actively replace thoughts and feelings that are counterproductive to that. Here are thoughts from the story, their impact on feelings and how they can be changed.

Negative thoughts	Negative feelings	Powerful thoughts	Powerful feelings
What does this mean for me?	Nervous Anxious	*How can I make this work for me?*	Optimistic
I can't believe they are springing the news on us like this! They can't be serious!	Fearful Suspicious	*I need to understand more about the change. Who can I talk to that can support and help with this, and give answers?*	Eager Encouraged
This could affect me badly, it could impact my pay and maybe I wouldn't be able to send the kids on the school trip to Italy. And that holiday we have booked! How are they thinking this is going to work?	Guilty Disappointed	*I am sure this will all be fine, we will work out how this can work for the best for all of us.*	Determined Bold
What if people are not fair but vindictive?	Doubtful Skeptical	*People will get used to the new process and using it fairly will become the norm. I will continue to do the best job I can.*	Certain Secure

▶

Negative thoughts	Negative feelings	Powerful thoughts	Powerful feelings
Will I be punished just because I didn't see eye to eye with one of my colleagues and they decide to mark me down? This is crazy!	Powerless	*I can take control of the way I behave in this and act with integrity.*	Credible Satisfied
I have bad feelings about this.	Despair	*I am going to find the positive in this change and make it work for me. It will be better.*	Enthusiastic Hopeful

Summary

Communicate more

Managing change starts and ends with communication. Whenever you think you've communicated enough, you probably need to communicate some more. The key is to make it interactive and involving, to listen, talk and involve others.

Communicate, communicate, communicate – and then some.

Awareness of the change curve

Help your team members understand the predictability of human reaction at the various stages of the change curve. The awareness of the change curve makes change less threatening – 'it's not just me that feels this way'. Each stage is needed, but how long someone stays at each stage and how far the energy and productivity drops, can be managed and kept to a minimum.

For more ideas on how to manage the change curve, go to http://www.leadingteamsbook.com/

Transformational change

Transformational change happens at a behavioural level. Unless you get people to change behaviours, no real change will be possible. When putting together change plans, focus on the behaviours that will make a difference, what people need to do differently to achieve the results.

Reflection questions for the reader

■ How well do we manage change in this team? Can we do better?

■ How do my own reactions to change, positive or negative, impact my team members?

■ How can we be more proactive about change as a team?

■ How can I involve my team members more in any upcoming changes?

■ How am I considering where others are on the change curve compared to me in times of change?

Self-assessment

After you have implemented the solutions in this chapter, answer these questions again to see the progress you have made.

How would you rate the following in your team?

	1 Very poor	2 Poor	3 Just OK	4 Good	5 Excellent
Effectiveness of change implementation					
Acceptance of change					
Dealing with change					
Proactively leading change					

How do you get a team working together 'all for one and one for all'?

- Increasing respect and support in the team
- Increasing commitment between team members

'The strength of the team is each individual member. The strength of each member is the team.'

Phil Jackson.

Self-assessment

Before reading the chapter, do the following quick self-assessment.

How would you rate the following in your team?

	1	2	3	4	5
	Very poor	Poor	Just OK	Good	Excellent
We are 'all for one and one for all'					
Respect for each other					
Support of each other					
Awareness of team dynamics					

Everything's in hand, or is it?

The weekly conference call with the team was in full swing.

'So, where are we with the plans for the project in Düsseldorf, Fred?' queried Davide.

'We are progressing to plan. Everything's in hand, there are no issues to report.' As usual, Fred's response was brief and to the point, and always positive.

Jon was slightly uncomfortable. He knew Fred better than a few months ago but he was still questioning if he was getting the whole story any time Fred opened his mouth. *It was always good and it couldn't always be good! Is he hiding something again?* Jon decided to speak up.

'Fred, when I was in Düsseldorf last week, I attended a project meeting where there was some concern over the end-of-quarter deadline for Phase 2. To me it sounded like it's not really going to plan.'

Silence followed, accompanied by some crackling sounds on the line.

After a few moments, Fred responded, his voice a bit louder than before.

'Actually Jon, I think you've got that wrong. Let's be honest, I think you may have misinterpreted what was said and this is probably down to not quite knowing how we do things in Germany.'

Even though he sounded in control, Fred was inwardly worried that Jon's experience out-trumped his own and it made him feel as if he had to demonstrate his competence and power. He cleared his throat and continued to explain why everything was good, the process they were going through, while throwing in some local technical reference to show that he had everything under control.

Far away, Jon was shaking his head, thinking: *There's no point in saying anything. He's just doing his own thing. What happened to the team?*

Davide started to recognise that there was a pattern to these calls. More often than not, someone felt the need to beat their chest and prove how great they were. This was clearly not anywhere near the level of teamwork he wanted to see. Getting to know each other, which they had started to do, had not been enough.

Meanwhile, unbeknown to the others, two other team members were instant messaging each other as usual. They were gossiping about how unnecessary Fred's pompous rant was and how annoying it was that Jon had to ask the question, which provoked the rant. *Now it was all just going to take longer*, they lamented.

Exploring the problem

Conference calls can be challenging in their own right. They are great tools, but to work well they have to be both disciplined and focused, and have appropriate active involvement. Virtual teams, where team members are not all in the same place, are dependent on this critical communication tool and have to make it work well.

Honest response

In this call, Fred's reluctance to share the whole story makes Jon suspicious. As he doesn't get a totally honest response, it makes him feel distant from Fred. It drives them apart as team members.

The fact that two other team members are instant messaging each other, about the behaviours shown by Jon and Fred is another indication of how disparate the team is. All of this creates an 'us and them' mentality, which is detrimental to team unity.

Isolation

When the distancing happens through these behaviours *and* the team is not located together, it creates a sense of isolation. People feel alone and, when they feel alone, they fend for themselves. It's no longer about the greater good, if it ever was, it's about setting their own individual course. And that's not what teams are all about.

Imposter syndrome

As the team is located in several different countries, lack of awareness of cultural differences can drive a team apart, which is hinted at in Fred's comment about Jon not understanding how things work in Germany.

Fred feels inferior to Jon. When Jon challenges him, he feels like he has to make himself look better than Jon, and the way he does it is to stick to his original comment rather than admitting that there was a problem. He suffers from the 'imposter syndrome', where the sufferer is fearful that people will find out that he is not as good as he sets himself up to be. The imposter syndrome does not necessarily happen at a conscious level, but it drives the behaviours that we can see.

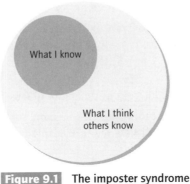

Figure 9.1 The imposter syndrome

Fears are not uncommon in the workplace. The most common fears we see are:

- **Fear of failure**: This fear of making mistakes is likely to drive a controlling behaviour, thinking you have to be 'perfect'.

- **Fear of rejection**: This is the fear that others will not like you and will push you away. It is likely to drive behaviours of wanting to please others and avoiding conflicts.

Both fears, although natural, are not conducive to effective teamwork. In great teams people feel safe and are able to be open and transparent with each other without fear of negative consequences.

The reasons for team members not working together 'all for one and one for all'

A gossip culture

Team members can have a habit of speculating and jumping to conclusions. This typically happens behind 'closed doors' and is the opposite to transparent and respectful communication. And once this habit is in place, it can gain a life of its own, where speculation leads to more speculation, rumours and exaggerated guesses.

Team members don't see the benefits

Team members may not have experienced strong, fully supportive teamwork before and therefore are not aware of the benefits it could bring.

The team is not all located in the same place

When teams are not all based in the same physical workplace, it can be harder to feel like a team or know how to work together across different locations.

'Us and them' mentality

Cliques and sub-groups are not uncommon in teams, but they do nothing for proper teamwork. The reason they are created though is that it's often easier for individuals to find allegiances in one or two people than a whole team, unless they are helped to do so.

Team constellation changes

A team may only stay intact for so long. Natural employee turn-over means that team members leave and others join. These changes can make it more challenging to bond and gel as a team.

Team members are not respectful or supportive towards each other

Unhelpful behaviour towards each other within a team, such as withholding information, going behind each other's backs, exclusion and bullying, simply drives a team apart.

Team members think they have all the answers themselves

Many employees think the leader has to have all the answers – and even if they don't, the leader often thinks this anyway. This is also true for people in general; we can be reluctant to admit to not knowing something, especially when we think *others* think we should know.

Team members not understanding each other's cultures

Everyone has their own frame of reference, based on cultural values and habits, as well as experience and personality. Without valuable knowledge of other cultures and backgrounds, it can be difficult for team members to understand and accept each other and open up for mutual teamwork. This can also happen when people have different styles.

> 'We don't see things as they are, we see them as we are.'
> Anais Nin

The impact of not working together 'all for one and one for all'

- Team members are inefficient, individually and as a team.
- Gossiping and an 'us and them' mentality make people feel uncertain and guarded.
- Team members can feel lonely and isolated. This, and a perceived lack of loyalty, can make team members less inclined to stay in the team.
- Everyone fends for themselves.
- When cultures or styles are misunderstood, team members can feel disrespected, left out and not understood or listened to.

The impact on the business, customers, employees and stakeholders

Productivity and financial results are impacted when teams are gossiping, which wastes time and causes insecurity and again inefficiency.

> Wayne was promoted to become the leader of his former peers. Two of his peers had also applied for the job, but had not been successful. Wayne had always had a good relationship with his peers and had 'grown up' with many of the team. After a while he realised that the others were having a hard time relating to him as their superior. He started to notice that the others had become more reserved towards him and conversations stopped when he showed up. One day he overheard how two members were complaining about him having made a decision without consulting them, given they had relevant knowledge he lacked. It made him acutely aware that this perceived competition was taking focus away from their job while affecting morale. Time and energy was wasted, while they were all also moaning about having too much to do.

This example highlights a common problem, which can drive a team apart if not addressed, and the climate as well as business results can be affected.

When individuals feel isolated and get demotivated, absenteeism can affect both customer experience and the bottom line. This feeling of isolation means employees can be less inclined to stay in the organisation, creating higher employee turnover, which absolutely impacts the customer experience. It takes time to bring new employees up to speed and contribute to a high standard.

Working in isolation is the opposite to team spirit.

Team spirit was perfectly portrayed in Alexandre Dumas' famous story of *The Three Musketeers*. Their motto, 'All for one and one for all', is as relevant today as it was in the 1800s when the book was written.

If you look closely at the winning soccer teams in the World Cup, for example, they typically epitomise this kind of team spirit, as great teams put the team ahead of themselves. There is no one star that the team stands and falls with. The fact that everyone plays an important role, coupled with the faith that great results can be achieved together, is at the centre of these footballers' team spirit. This means that even if one of their best players is missing, the team is still as strong. This is interesting as this is not necessarily true for most teams, where some team members have a perceived or real 'higher status' than their teammates. Others therefore feel inferior and potentially less valuable and important, and the star's absence at best worries and at worst cripples the team's performance.

With great team spirit everyone is willing to 'sacrifice' themselves for the team. They know that their shared mission is bigger than their personal agenda. And they know that they have a responsibility towards their team members to always behave in a manner that is conducive with their target mission. In fact, in many sports teams, you wouldn't even be allowed to play if you *weren't* thinking 'all for one and one for all'!

In a work example, that kind of team spirit may mean that a team member cancels a meeting with a senior mentor, even though that would be helpful for his/her own career, in order to step in for a team member who has been taken ill or fallen behind for some reason. The team goes before the individual and as a result the team has greater results and success, which ultimately also means the individual has greater success. It's a win–win mentality.

Solutions

Getting a team to embody the team spirit of 'all for one and one for all' takes time, energy and effort. This whole book outlines solutions that can make this a reality. What all solutions have in common is making it possible for team members to know, like and trust each other, and to want to achieve more because they are a team. This kind of climate can be created.

Let's get specific on how to do it.

Solution 1: Stop gossiping and making assumptions

Negative gossip is always unhelpful. It creates barriers. At the same time, however, speculation is natural as a way to make sense of what you hear or observe. There's a fine a line between unhealthy gossip and healthy speculation.

The best way to stop gossip is not to engage with it, and to ask those who gossip to go and talk to the right sources rather than going behind their backs. Don't collude with gossiping behaviour. If you or others have concerns that make you speculate, talk openly, ask questions, get clarification. If gossip isn't stopped, it becomes a culture; people think it's OK to do it, and this can become addictive.

Solution 2: Highlight reasons and benefits

Make sure people see the reasons and benefits of working as ONE team. To create shared ownership, get the team to brainstorm what the reasons and benefits are, or could be, of being a team. Once there are compelling reasons, teamwork becomes a 'no-brainer', it would be silly not to! To further embed this conviction, share stories of other teams who have achieved more because they have embraced teamwork. Sports teams are a great metaphor for this.

Solution 3: Virtual teams – create closeness like in onsite teams

When your team members are located in different locations, a lot of the natural teaming that can happen in day-to-day conversations and interactions is not there, and focused effort will be needed to create team spirit. Talk to the team and make them aware of how this can be done, and ask for their ideas too. Here are some ideas and considerations:

Face-to-face meetings	If possible, bring the team together face-to-face for kick-offs, wrap-ups and celebrations, as well as conflict resolution. At an individual level, hold performance appraisals face-to-face whenever possible.
Create a team charter	A team charter gives the complete picture of a team, what it does and how it will do it. This makes it easier for a team to operate and be successful and is a must for a team who wants to maximise their success. Work as a team to create a crystal clear team charter, which outlines the team's purpose, goals and plans, resources needed, roles and responsibilities and operating guidelines (how we will work together). A team charter that is created by everyone, is owned by everyone and therefore is carried out by everyone.
Conference calls	Always have an agenda for the call, so everyone knows what to expect and can prepare. Keep in mind that it's absolutely OK to have creative, open-ended brainstorming meetings over the phone too. Make sure everyone has photos of all team members, which you can look at when the respective people are talking. Or you can use equipment that allows for visual links into the conference call. This creates more of a face-to-face feeling. Take turns facilitating the calls.
Make use of technology	Have online chat rooms where team members can interact with each other in a more informal way. This can be a quick way of updating each other on things that everyone needs to be aware of. Another way of using a chat room is to have a 'virtual coffee morning or tea break' where team members can have a quick break with their colleagues at a given time.
Create work sub-teams	Where it makes sense, form sub-teams to work on specific initiatives for a given time, to maximise exchange of ideas and experience as well as building team spirit.

Solution 4: Get to 'we' talk

Make a habit of using 'we' talk. When you talk about the team, with the team or outside it, use words that demonstrate your commitment to the team, and encourage others to do the same. Here are some examples:

▪ We have some great opportunities to ...

▪ Together we can ...

▪ How can we solve this together?

▪ What are the next steps we should take?

▪ This is what I will do for us ...

Solution 5: Create transferable team skills set

Whatever you learn in a team, you can take to the next team. Teamwork is never wasted. If you're in a team, you might as well throw yourself in completely and embrace the teamwork and the learning it gives. You can then go to the next team with the knowledge of how to build and maintain a strong team, whether you are a leader or a team member. Make use of your transferable team skill set.

Solution 6: Talk respectfully to each other

It's not just about what you say, it's much more about how you say it. Think about how you talk to or respond to a colleague. One example could be having to say no to a colleague who is asking for your help. You may want to help but you also need to leave as you are picking up your child from school. You can either just say, 'No, I can't do it' or you can say, 'I'd really like to help. Unfortunately I am just about to leave to pick up my son Peter, he's waiting outside school. Can I help you tomorrow?' Which answer would you rather be the receiver of? So as you can see, it's not the what, it's all about the how.

Another aspect of respectful language is reflected in how you give each other feedback on both strengths and development areas. Peer-to-peer coaching is a very powerful way to develop and grow as individuals and as a team. Give feedback with the other person's best interest in mind, share your specific observations and the impact of what you have observed, positively or constructively. Show that you care; use words, tone of voice and body language that convey a message of genuine interest and goodwill.

Solution 7: The answers are in the team

Everyone brings their knowledge, ideas and answers to a team. No one can have all the answers, which is why great teams make sure they involve everyone in creative processes and fact finding. Encourage team members to let their guards down and willingly admit that they don't know everything, and are open to the input of others, not being threatened by any perceived superiority of others.

Solution 8: Learn about and use the cultures in the team

Globalisation means that more and more teams are becoming multi-cultural, with members from different cities, regions and countries. This is a great source of diversity, which can add to the team's knowledge and expertise. Take time to learn about each other's cultures, looking for the opportunities in the differences rather than the threats of unfamiliarity. Keep asking yourself the question: What different backgrounds do we have in the team that might be useful and/or give unique insight right now? By doing so, you will add to your team's Cultural Intelligence (CQ), which can be said to be a subset to Emotional Intelligence (EQ) or Social Intelligence (SQ).

Solution 9: Rally together to overcome a shared challenge

There's nothing quite like a challenge to bring people together. It's often said that in times of crises, people stand side by side. Why wait for a crisis to work together? Start working together now and get your team focused on the shared challenge you have. Learn from any crisis that you have been through and take that learning into your everyday teamwork.

Let's have a look at what Davide, Fred and Jon could have done instead, had they deployed these solutions.

The weekly conference call with the team was in full swing.

'So, where are we with the plans for the project in Düsseldorf, Fred?' queried Davide.

'We are progressing to plan. Everything's in hand, there are no issues to report.' As usual, Fred's response was brief and to the point, and always positive.

Jon was slightly uncomfortable. He knew Fred better than a few months ago but he still was questioning if he was getting the whole story any time that Fred opened his mouth. Jon decided to speak up.

'Fred, I'm sure that things are moving along fine. Let me just share though; when I was in Düsseldorf last week, I attended a project meeting where there was some concern over the end-of-quarter deadline for Phase 2. Maybe I don't quite know all the ins and outs of operations in Germany, so I was hoping we could have a look at where we are with this together'.

Fred responded.

'I appreciate you asking. There are some aspects of how we operate that may be the reason for the discrepancy. Let me explain.' Fred continued to share the whole story. When he was done, Jon spoke again.

'Thanks, that was really helpful actually. I've learnt something new today. And it's given me some ideas for how we could work on our next project. I think we should get some more collaboration going between our different locations, to share best practices *and* challenge the status quo.'

Fred was pleased that Jon had expressed gratitude and admitted that he had learnt from Fred. It felt good and it made him willing to explore the idea of collaboration.

Davide nodded to himself, impressed with how his direct reports were taking shared responsibility without him having to be the one to ask for it. Yes, things were starting to progress nicely with the team.

Behaviours of team and leader

Under 'Solutions' above, we have listed a number of 'how to' actions. These solutions work best when carried out with these supporting 'how to' behaviours. The actions on their own will get you only so far. With the right behaviours you can get a team working together more effectively, 'all for one and one for all'.

'How to' solutions	'How to' behaviours	How the behaviours make the difference
Stop gossiping and making assumptions.	Being honest Being friendly	When you are honest in a friendly way, you encourage others to be the same, which makes it impossible for gossiping to work.
Highlight reasons and benefits.	Being curious Listening	With a curious, open mind you can find reasons together. You can invite ideas from your team members, showing that you value their input, which makes it compelling to work with you.
Virtual teams: create closeness like in onsite teams.	Being observant Listening	Being attuned to your team members, listening to what's being said and observing how people act and react, makes you more aware of what the team needs to be as close as possible.
Get to 'we' talk.	Being inclusive	Always think of yourself as a member of the team; this makes inclusiveness simple and 'we' talk becomes automatic.
Create transferable team skills set.	Being curious	With a curious mind you will look for team learning opportunities and how you can build the best possible team wherever you are and whatever team you are in.
Talk respectfully to each other.	Being friendly	By being friendly and having your team members best interest in mind, it helps to put your messages across in such a way that others will want to listen openly to what you are saying.
The answers are in the team.	Being curious	By being curious you see and show the value in your team members' thoughts, experience and knowledge. You do have all the answers in the team, you just have to find them.

▶

'How to' solutions	'How to' behaviours	How the behaviours make the difference
Learn about and use the cultures in the team.	Being curious Being open-minded	Being open-minded makes you listen and value what is different to you, encouraging team members to make the most of the fact that everyone is uniquely different with different input to offer.
Rally together to overcome a shared challenge.	Being determined	Show your determination and energy as a way to convey your commitment to the team and the challenge you face.

Thoughts and feelings of team and leader

On average, a person experiences around 70.000 thoughts per day.[1] Many of those thoughts are habits that affect a person's mindset or outlook.

What we think affects how we feel, and how we feel affects how we think.

When wanting to get a team working together, 'all for one and one for all', actively replace thoughts and feelings that are counterproductive to that. Here are thoughts from the story, their impact on feelings and how they can be changed.

Negative thoughts	Negative feelings	Powerful thoughts	Powerful feelings
Is he hiding something again?	Suspicious	*I wonder what else he might know. I will encourage him to share by asking.*	Curious
I worry that Jon's experience out-trumps mine (he's better than me).	Fear	*I have something valuable to contribute, as does Jon.*	Confidence
There's no point in saying anything. He's just doing his own thing.	Hopeless	*It's always important to speak up in a respectful way. That's how we progress.*	Hope Confidence

▶

Negative thoughts	Negative feelings	Powerful thoughts	Powerful feelings
How unnecessary Fred's pompous rant is!	Frustration	*I am open and non-judgmental to others. I listen, and challenge if needed.*	Calm Confidence
Now it is all just going to take longer.	Hopeless	*This conversation could be valuable too.*	Hope Confidence

Summary

Honour your time

Getting a team to be like the three musketeers – 'all for one and one for all' – is not a utopia. It is most definitely a possibility that all teams should consider. If you're in a team, you may as well *really* be in it. Working together side by side is about making the most of the fact that you are a team. It's about honouring your time and efforts at work by seeing yourself as a full-time member of the team, not just an individual contributor.

Get the whole team talking

Imagine how great it would feel to be part of a team where everyone is happy to do things for the good of the team and not just themselves. Get the whole team talking about the possibilities of excellent teamwork based on generosity and inclusion and start to reap the rewards.

Reflection questions for the reader

- How willing am I to admit to not having all the answers?
- How can I best show respect to my team members?
- What can I learn today from being a member of this team?
- How can we make our conference calls more interesting, effective and valuable?
- What is our key challenge right now, which we can all rally behind?
- What transferable team skills do I have?

Self-assessment

After you have implemented the solutions in this chapter, answer these questions again to see the progress you have made.

How would you rate the following in your team?

	1	2	3	4	5
	Very poor	Poor	Just OK	Good	Excellent
All for one and one for all					
Respect for each other					
Support of each other					
Awareness of team dynamics					

How do you get everyone going in the same direction?

- Increasing understanding of the team's common purpose
- Creating shared team ownership of goals
- Getting the team aligned towards a shared outcome

'Vision without action is merely a dream. Action without vision just passes the time. Vision with action can change the world.'

Joel Barker

Self-assessment

Before reading the chapter, do the following quick self-assessment.

How would you rate the following in your team?

	1 Very poor	2 Poor	3 Just OK	4 Good	5 Excellent
Clarity of common purpose					
Shared team responsibility					
Understanding of each other's roles and responsibility					
Going in the same direction is a priority					

A team thrown together

It was time for another team re-organisation. Ted found himself reporting to a new manager again. It was his third in two years.

I don't mind the new reporting line, Donald is not a bad leader, but it means I'm now forced into a team with Trevor! It really doesn't make sense to me that we should now somehow work together. We have absolutely nothing in common. In fact, I don't think he even comes close to understanding or representing what my team does, so it feels false, forced and uncomfortable. And now Donald wants us to have some kind of shared team event. I need to talk to him about all this; it just doesn't make sense.

Ted's thoughts were interrupted by Donald's very timely entrance into his office.

▶ 'Hi Ted. I'm glad I caught you. I need to check some possible dates with you for the planned team event.'

Ted looked down rather than meeting Donald's gaze. 'OK' he muttered.

Unperturbed, Donald continued. 'I want it to be 10 February. Does that work for you?'

'Not sure I can make the tenth. February overall isn't a good month for me.'

'Well, it needs to be February. What date *can* you do?'

'I don't want to seem uncooperative, but I don't actually see the point in a team event with Trevor's team. The only thing we have in common is reporting into you. That doesn't make us a team, not in my mind anyway.' Ted paused.

Donald hadn't even considered that there might be resistance to his plans of bringing together his direct reports.

'What's the problem? You *do* both report into me and that makes you part of my team. So the team event is going ahead. So can you please let me know what dates you can do in February?'

'Well, I could maybe make the 12th work,' Ted admitted. 'But what are we going to do? What's the point of this event?'

Donald was getting annoyed and snapped: 'Oh come on, Ted. This is how it is. We have to be a team because you all report into me. Let's just get on with it! This session will help us do that. We'll all get to know each other better and that will be that.' His tone indicated that the conversation was over.

When Donald had left, Ted was even more frustrated than he had been before their conversation.

I don't want to be directly associated with Trevor. My team is very different to his. I'm struggling to see what we have in common.

Exploring the problem

Ted is clearly struggling to see any connection between his new peer and himself.

He understands that the organisational change has thrown them together but he doesn't understand what makes them a team.

Donald thinks Ted and Trevor *are* a team because they report into him. This is not enough for Ted who feels more frustrated after their talk.

Feeling superior

Ted feels superior to Trevor and his team. He doesn't think Trevor represents the same values or holds himself to the same high standards as Ted does. Therefore he worries that being associated with Trevor will negatively impact his image and reputation in the organisation. This makes him less cooperative than he would normally be.

No shared purpose

Ted can't see what Trevor and he have in common, and therefore he rejects the idea of them being a team. There is no obvious shared purpose for them both, or their teams.

They are not working on the same things and they are not heading in the same direction.

When team members are not aware of a shared purpose, there will be no obvious reason to work together.

Donald needs Ted and Trevor to be a team, for his own practical purposes, but he is unable to give a convincing reason for this, or just hasn't considered that he needs one.

The reasons for team members not going in the same direction

They don't know where to go

If there is no common purpose and direction, people will do their own thing, focus on their specific tasks or do very little, as they'll have no drive to go anywhere beyond just getting the job done.

There is a conflict of roles and responsibilities

If roles and responsibilities have been created more or less in isolation, any connections between the roles are unlikely to have been explored enough. This may, for example, be the case if two teams merge and the lines of responsibility are blurred. This could mean that either too many people are taking responsibility for a task, or no one is, both of which undermine any sense of going in the same direction.

Their goals are not aligned

If there are no team goals, people will only be working on their own individual goals, which may be in conflict with those of their team members. This further feeds the feeling of not going in the same direction and creates a downward spiral into non-collaboration.

They don't understand their purpose

The purpose is either not known to them, or they don't feel the emotional bond that's needed to be able to truly understand it and act on it.

It's not obvious that they need to go in the same direction

A leader may assume that team members understand they should collaborate towards an outcome, instead of pointing it out explicitly to them. Many leaders leave that assumption at an implicit level, especially if it's clear to him/herself.

Team purpose and direction is not prioritised

Team purpose and direction is not discussed and hence not prioritised. Focus is given to the short term, the individual tasks in the here and now, rather than the team's reason to be.

They don't want to work together

There's a resistance to collaboration due to personality differences, current conflicts, having worked together before unsuccessfully, not knowing each other, not liking each other, not trusting each other and many other reasons. Previous bad experiences, where people have encountered each other, shape their opinions of each other. This colours their perception into the future, even though the current reality could be very different and the person could be different in this new context.

The resistance can also be a reaction to not feeling involved or having a say in the matter.

The impact of teams not going in the same direction

- It's demotivating and affects engagement levels. Team members then need to find other ways to be energised, which may turn them away from their work, and lead them to be distracted and to lose focus.

- It can create work/responsibility overlaps, extra work, duplication of work and inefficiencies. Unclear responsibilities mean that too much or too little is done.

- Team members may start making up their own purposes, which can be in conflict with those of other team members, driving them even further apart. People end up doing their own thing, being more influenced by self-interest than what's best for the company. They work in isolation, focused on their own needs. The effect is they are not looking out for each other within the team or supporting each other outside of the team. This can be seen as disloyalty.

The impact on the business, customers, employees and stakeholders

When employees are not aligned and not going in the same direction, the rework and low engagement and even employee turnover becomes costly to the organisation. Duplication of work and effort has a high impact on the bottom line too.

Michelle was on a conference call with her colleagues. A number of them were located in another office and mainly communicated via email and conference calls. The calls were made up of long monologues on results, which meant very little to her and she had often, in her mind, questioned the relevance of the calls. She found herself distracted by the new camera features on her mobile phone and started taking pictures of the scenery outside the window. She suddenly heard her name called out and forced herself back into the call and started reading through her update. Within a minute

▶

> ▶ or so one of her colleagues interrupted her and asked her why she was
> reporting on something that he had already covered. This was news
> to Michelle who had neither heard his update nor known that he was
> working on a similar initiative to her. She felt annoyed at herself for
> letting this happen. She was also feeling despondent about the time
> she had wasted doing the same work as someone else.

This example highlights two key issues. The team members are working in isolation, not knowing what the others are doing. They are also lacking a sense of shared direction and responsibility and therefore not taking a real interest in what is going on in the call.

When goals are not clearly connected, the leader will need to get involved, especially if goals are counterproductive to each other. This would not have been necessary if people within the team had been aware of their shared purpose and taken shared responsibility. It's a waste of the leader's time and it undermines the team's self-esteem.

Let's look at another example.

> A service organisation had a high employee turnover for a few years.
> Through exit interviews they identified that most of those who were
> leaving had experienced a feeling of 'no point' to their job. They
> reported feeling as if it was all just about meeting the numbers.
> They hadn't understood the bigger picture and the purpose of the
> organisation. This made the CEO painfully aware that they hadn't done
> a good job at communicating that their reason to be was to create a
> worry-free situation for the customers. Had the employees known this
> they could have had a purpose to their job and made their role bigger
> than just delivering the numbers. They would have connected to it at
> an emotional level and given their own job more meaning.

As this example shows, people respond to purposes. If employees can't see how they are contributing to something bigger than the task at hand, the job is often not as engaging and motivating as it could have been had the purpose been understood and bought into.

Solutions

Dr Martin Luther King famously said, 'I have a dream ...'. He didn't say, 'I have a strategic plan ...'. Joking aside, he had a dream, a vision of a better future (he possibly had a strategic plan as well, but that wasn't part of the communication message that became so famous). These two things are very different in nature and are appropriate and effective at different stages of progression. It's rare for people to get passionate about strategic plans, that's not their purpose, but dreams and visions can be compelling and engaging. Good visions have a few components in common. They are inspirational, they paint a believable and appealing picture of the future which people can feel, they engage both hearts and minds. Great visions help you experience what it will be like to get there; how it will feel, what it will look and sound like. They make people passionate and lead to actions that are practical.

It's the leader's role to rally people behind the compelling reason to be, the purpose, in order to achieve or at least aspire towards the vision. The vision gives meaning and purpose to what a team does.

To get the full power of a vision, you need awareness of the current reality too. If the vision is strong enough, it makes the team take the necessary actions to lead them there. The pull of the vision, when appealing enough, draws the team towards it. The natural tension between where you are as a team and where you want to go, is resolved.

This then helps in the creation of the strategic plan to move in the direction of the vision.

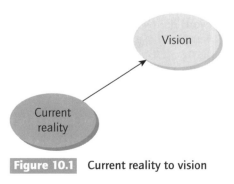

Figure 10.1   Current reality to vision

Research into human motivation, shows that purpose is one of the strongest factors for intrinsic motivation.[6] Purpose answers the question 'why' and gives meaning to what we do.

By getting your team to march in the same direction, you overcome the challenge of a disparate team.

Let's get specific on how to do it.

Solution 1: Create a vision

If there is no vision in place, you may want to create one. It's not an absolute must for a team to have their own vision (the vision of the organisation can be enough). However, if you want to create a team one, here's some food for thought.

A great vision is aspirational; you don't necessarily need to achieve it, but you need to continue to experience its pull. You might even argue that you *don't* want to achieve a vision, because then you would need to create a new one. Regardless, a vision is something that inspires you and moves you forward.

Here's a vision creation exercise to help you:

> Get a stack of magazines, scissors, glue, tape, post-it notes and a big flipchart. Have everyone go through the magazines and cut out any pictures or words that capture their attention as a representation of what the vision could be about. Ask them to simply focus on the future, what it will look, feel and sound like when you get to the vision. Stick the pictures onto the flipchart to make a collage. Ask each team member to explain why they have chosen the pictures and make the connections. As a team use this discussion to form the key words to create and describe the vision. Then, the team can wordsmith the vision using the key words from the discussions.

Here are some examples of potential team visions:

- To become the best service team in the industry
- To be the team where everyone wants to work
- To be the team that fully supports the organisation by helping each and every customer.

Solution 2: Identify the common purpose together

Closely linked to the vision is a team's purpose. A team's purpose is the reason to be, what they are here to do. Involve your team in identifying or clarifying the common purpose that you share. All teams have some shared purpose, the reason to be, that all team members need to both understand and buy into. By involving the team, rather than just telling them what it is, everyone becomes an owner of the purpose. The process can be fast-forwarded by having input from the team on what they think the purpose is through a climate study. A climate study is a simple process, that can look like this:

- **Step 1**: You interview each person.
- **Step 2**: You gather all of the interview notes and everyone's individual thoughts on the team and the purpose.
- **Step 3**: At the meeting you discuss the purpose and the outcomes of the Team Climate Study. As they already have a lot of input from the study, it helps them hit the ground running.

Solution 3: Make the purpose grounded

The purpose needs to be clear to all, actionable and tangible. It needs to be something that can be achieved. Making the purpose grounded is about creating the team map, explaining that 'because we do this, we are able to achieve what we are here to do, and we contribute directly to the vision and purpose of the organisation as a whole'. The team map makes the links for everyone and is a way of creating an overview for the team.

Solution 4: Clarify roles and responsibilities

Having clear roles and responsibilities for all team members makes the purpose even easier to take personal responsibility for. Here's an exercise you can do to make everyone aware of your individual responsibilities in the team:

Part 1: Take turns writing down your role and responsibility and ask others to write down what they think your role and responsibility is – and then check: is there a mismatch? If so, this may be another reason why you are not achieving alignment as a team.
Part 2: identify what people like doing – and re-allocate responsibilities based on that or put into place 'buddy systems' to allow people to share and teach others to do the things they themselves like doing. We are more likely to enjoy and do an excellent job on things we enjoy doing.

Solution 5: Create shared team responsibility

Individual responsibility is key, but so is shared responsibility. Discuss as a team what your shared responsibilities are – ultimately it's fulfilling your purpose. Each person needs to understand that he/she is responsible for the overall results of the team, not just their individual goals. One way of doing this is to make sure that all goals are aligned in some way, so that it's not even possible for someone to go for individual success without considering the rest of the team.

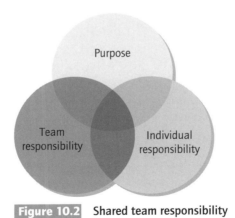

Figure 10.2   **Shared team responsibility**

Solution 6: Create a link

Even if there is a tenuous link between what team members do, like in the story of Ted and Trevor, you can create that link and make it stronger. You can actively look for what people have in common through their contribution to the organisation and the benefits they can have from being a team, thereby giving them a shared purpose.

Solution 7: Use a crisis to show you the way

During a crisis, team members are forced to work together to solve the issue. If your team experiences a crisis (e.g. a system break-down, bad press, big customer issue), then use the learning that crisis gives. Look at how you did it, what worked and what didn't. Identify how you need to work together, how you can be better aligned for successful results. Don't wait for another crisis to work together – work together like that every day.

Solution 8: Give strengths-based feedback

Be observant and recognise how each person contributes to the team's work. Look for strengths in others and give them that feedback. Strengths-based feedback is when you share a specific observation you have made when a person's strength was used AND clearly contributed to fulfilling the team's purpose. The more information you can give, the more helpful it will be. It could sound something like this:

> 'I have noticed several times that you are very good at piecing information together, making sense of seemingly disparate bits of data. And the way you did it today was particularly good. In our meeting, you proactively offered to share what you saw and were able to explain it in such a way that we could all see it too. As a result, we quickly got a shared view of a new perspective on how to solve the issue with the new customer requirements. It was great – please keep doing it!'

Telling people about their strengths, rather than telling them what they have done wrong, reinforces those strengths and helps them to use the strengths more. When hearing about their strengths, people connect with them as part of their own purpose which can then connect to the team purpose too.

Solution 9: Create a team charter

A team charter is a document that describes the purpose, framework and agreements of the team – many of the solutions listed above. The team creates it themselves, hence making it a powerful and a visual shared commitment. It typically at least includes:

- Purpose and clear links to organisation's vision and purpose
- Expectations and goals
- Roles and responsibilities
- Skills and expertise needed (to fulfil purpose)
- Resources needed (to fulfil purpose)
- Operating guidelines: behaviours and how the team will work together (to fulfil purpose)
- Signed agreement.

Let's have a look at what Ted and Donald could have done instead, had they deployed these solutions.

Donald was thinking hard. In the latest re-organisation he had been asked to take on two senior leaders who had previously not worked together and on the surface of it didn't seem like they had much in common. But somehow he needed to make it work.

Now that I think about it though, there are some great opportunities in them being on my team. Ted's international experience paired with Trevor's knowledge of the customer could help us look at our client communication in a new creative way. I will sit them both down and explain how both their teams contribute to the overall client experience and ask for their input. I think we can break new ground here.

He picked up the phone and called Ted first.

'Hi Ted. I'm glad I caught you. I have some interesting ideas that I would like to share with you. The change in reporting line, which I know has initially resulted in some raised eyebrows, is showing some great new opportunities for us that I think you will like. Can we meet and talk?'

Ted's interest was piqued. 'Absolutely – do you have any time today? Let's get together.'

Behaviours of team and leader

Under 'Solutions' above, we have listed a number of 'how to' actions. These solutions work best when carried out with these supporting 'how to' behaviours. The actions on their own, will get you only so far.

'How to' solutions	'How to' behaviours	How the behaviours make the difference
Create a vision.	Be inspired	When you feel inspired, others can feel that inspiration and be encouraged to make the vision happen. Behaviour breeds behaviour, so if you are inspired others will be too.
Identify the common purpose together.	Be encouraging Be collaborative	We all want to know that what we do makes a difference, so encouraging people to create a common purpose together, makes them feel part of something bigger. They will want to be connected to something they personally can relate to.
Make the purpose grounded.	Be pragmatic	If the purpose is grounded and realistic team members will feel it is achievable and go 'the extra mile'.
Shared team responsibility.	Be inclusive	Everyone wants to feel included and involved and important. Sharing responsibility across the team gains buy in and enjoyment.
Create a link.	Be persuasive	Encourage and persuade team members to see the links they have to each other – make it compelling. This means you explicitly help them to make the connections along the way.
Use a crisis to show you the way.	Be inventive	By reflecting and learning from a crisis you are creating a learning culture which allows for people to be more creative in their day to day work.
Give strengths-based feedback.	Be kind, thoughtful, caring	By positively reinforcing strengths you are encouraging people to use what they are good at in the team. This gets people motivated.
Create a team charter.	Be interested	You are gaining commitment by being interested in the team and spending time creating the 'how to' operate as a team as well as the 'what to do'.

Thoughts and feelings of team and leader

On average, a person experiences around 70.000 thoughts per day.[1] Many of those thoughts are habits that affect a person's mindset or outlook.

What we think affects how we feel, and how we feel affects how we think.

When wanting a team to go in the same direction, together, actively replace thoughts and feelings that are counterproductive to that. Here are thoughts from the story, their impact on feelings and how they can be changed.

Negative thoughts	Negative feelings	Powerful thoughts	Powerful feelings
We have absolutely nothing in common.	Animosity	*I wonder what we could have in common? I'd like to find out.*	Curiosity Hopefulness
It really doesn't make sense to me that we should now somehow work together.	Frustration	*I'm sure it makes sense that we should work together. Let's find a way.*	Hopefulness
I don't want to seem uncooperative, but I don't see the point in a team event with Trevor's team.	Frustration	*I am cooperative and I will make the team event worthwhile attending.*	Determination
My association with Trevor can damage my image and reputation.	Fear	*I am in charge of my own image and my reputation.*	Confidence

Summary

Reason to be

For a team to walk in the same direction, they need to know where they are going or contributing to (vision) and why (purpose). This kind of clarity provides the framework and 'reason to be' that can really rally a team to work together towards goals that fulfil their purpose.

Remember that visions need to be compelling and purposes meaningful. People respond to the importance in both of these and the sense of making a difference to someone or something. A great example of this is the janitor at NASA who expressed that his job was to put people in space. He was able to see how important his job was in contributing to something that he thought was important and he could rally behind.

Time to focus on purpose

Time needs to be spent on this as early as possible in a team's existence. It also needs to be reviewed and recommitted to at regular intervals, when goals are set or adjusted, and when new team members join. A clear vision and joint purpose also provides a great framework for new employees, which can enable them to more quickly see the meaning in their job and how they can contribute.

Reflection questions for the reader

- ■ Would my team benefit from having a specific team vision?
- ■ Do we all know what our team's purpose is?
- ■ How do we need to work to best achieve our purpose?
- ■ What crisis have we been through that we could learn from?
- ■ How clear are the shared team responsibilities?

Self-assessment

After you have implemented the solutions in this chapter, answer these questions again to see the progress you have made.

How would you rate the following in your team?

	1 Very poor	2 Poor	3 Just OK	4 Good	5 Excellent
Clarity of common purpose					
Shared team responsibility					
Understanding each other's roles and responsibility					
Going in the same direction is a priority					

'If you want to build a ship, don't drum up people together to collect wood and don't assign them tasks and work, but rather teach them to long for the endless immensity of the sea.'
Antoine de Saint-Exupery

Straight-talking summary

This book is all about the simple things that make a team work well or even great, if you implement *all* the solutions. But it's like everything else, it only works if you do. So whatever ideas and solutions you have picked up as you have gone through this book – implement them. To help you, here are the headlines for each of the 'how to' solutions:

Challenge 1: How do you build trust?

Encourage your team members to talk.

Disclosure breeds disclosure, leading to greater openness.

If openness is lacking where you work, you can decide what you are willing and prepared to share.

You must spend time getting to know each other.

Explain why it's so important to know each other in order to work well together.

Keep promises.

Stop sticking your head in the sand (if you are)!

Challenge 2: How do you overcome conflicts or tensions?

Communicate, communicate, communicate.

Get together and ask constructive questions.

Assume positive intent.

Step into someone else's shoes.

Connect up team members' goals.

Let go of the need to be right.

Work on self-esteem.

Voice disagreement in a good way.

Challenge 3: How do you encourage everyone to share relevant information with each other?

It starts with you!

Make people aware of the effect.

Create and run 'sharing PODS' (Power Of Dynamic Sharing).

Link to the big picture.

Celebrate successes of when it's worked and delivered results.

Dare to share.

Challenge 4: How do you create engagement?

Role-model personal *response-ability*.

Clearly communicate the team's purpose and everyone's role in it.

Tell people how they are doing.

Get members working on innovative new ways of doing the job.

Be genuinely interested in your team members.

Have ongoing development discussions.

Celebrate success. Make it contagious.

Build team self-esteem.

Challenge 5: How do you create transparency and respect?

Tell the truth.

Reward transparency.

Leaders = role models.

Actively reach out to stakeholders.

Answer questions transparently.

Have a value of transparency.

Make transparency mandatory.

Challenge 6: How do you encourage long-term thinking?

Balance short- and long-term reporting.

Develop people's ability to think long-term.

Study the competition and the marketplace.

Be a 'time owl'.

Set team goals and decide rewards.

Communicate the overall purpose.

Invest in team time.

Take a long-term view on your team members.

Make the big picture understandable.

Challenge 7: How do you create a team that delivers and is well perceived?

Performance management.

Create a success habit.

Take responsibility.

Reframe learnings into better solutions.

Ask for feedback to understand perception.

Manage your reputation.

Build your team's brand.

Challenge 8: How do you get a team to manage change effectively?

Create a strategy and communication plan.

Slow down.

Positively reinforce strengths.

Communicate the change curve.

Recognise that you are not at the same stage of the change curve as others.

Demonstrate emotional intelligence.

Communicate, communicate, communicate.

Know that people are convinced in different ways.

Team decision-making.

Challenge 9: How do you get people working together 'all for one and one for all'?

Stop gossiping and making assumptions.

Highlight reasons and benefits.

Virtual teams: create closeness as in onsite teams.

Get to 'we' talk.

Create transferable team skills set.

Talk respectfully to each other.

The answers are in the team.

Learn about and use the cultures in the team.

Rally together to overcome a shared challenge.

Challenge 10: How do you get everyone going in the same direction?

Create a vision.

Identify the common purpose together.

Make the purpose grounded.

Shared team responsibility.

Create a link.

Use a crisis to show you the way.

Give strengths-based feedback.

Create a team charter.

Regardless of what team challenges you face, keep this in mind: if you want to achieve real, lasting change, pay particular attention to behaviours (*how* you implement these solutions).

How we behave and conduct ourselves has an impact on others, creating a ripple effect.

It's when we change our day-to-day behaviours that we can achieve transformational change.

Your Team Tool Kit on how to run a team workshop

Here is your handy Team Tool Kit, which you can use if you want to run a two-day workshop with your team, to fast-forward teamwork and results. The basis of the workshop is around getting the team members to know each other better, at a deeper level, and to create/clarify the shared purpose and clear way of working together, going forward. If you can only spend one day, adjust the agenda based on your desired outcomes for the session.

What to do before the workshop

Plan and do your research

Review your organisation's vision and the company values: how are people expected to behave/operate? What are the long- and short-term strategies, goals, plans? Who are the main competitors? What's the current market situation, threats and opportunities?

Then consider where your team fits into the overall picture and how you contribute to the vision. Review any data about the team: employee engagement studies, goal achievement, challenges, etc. Decide what you want to get out of the team workshop, the objectives.

Set the date

Make sure the date works for everyone, so that each team member feels important to the success of the event. Make sure all team members will be able to attend, because a team journey needs to include the right people.

Choose the venue

In-house or offsite? If budgets allow it, we recommend offsite as it keeps the team focused on the task at hand, rather than their normal work. For example, people tend to go back to their desk at lunchtime if the event is in-house, checking email and getting into work tasks.

Communicate

Explain to the team what the purpose of the team workshop is, when and where it will happen and what will be expected of them (e.g. full participation, an open mind etc.).

Pre-work

Give team members some pre-work to prepare. This should include some kind of reflection exercise where everyone reflects on their own strengths and development areas, what they enjoy the most about their work, how they contribute to the success of the team or something similar. Before you decide what to go for, carefully consider what outcome you are looking for and choose the individual reflection subjects that will be most valuable and relevant.

What to do at the workshop

This two-day agenda gives you some ideas on the contents you should consider.

What	How	Rough timings and other considerations
Welcome and introduction to the event	Go through purpose, objectives, agenda, expectations.	20–30 minutes
Introductions of team members	Take turns sharing something about yourselves that the others don't know – include personal things such as interests, hobbies, etc. Also ask each team member to share what they hope/intend to get out of the workshop (to create a sense of responsibility for outcomes).	20–40 minutes For more ideas, review the solutions in Chapter 1

▶

What	How	Rough timings and other considerations
Create agreement on principles/guidelines for the event	Discuss what's OK and not OK during the workshop (e.g. no phones, let everyone talk, come back on time after breaks, confidentiality, etc.).	10–20 minutes
Share and review individual pre-work	Let each person share their pre-work, to deepen understanding of each team member about each team member.	40–80 minutes
Give each other feedback on what's been shared from the pre-work	This is a great way to start sharing both positive and constructive feedback. If the team is new to feedback, concentrate on the positive, recognising and reinforcing each person's valuable contribution to the team.	40–80 minutes Use the TOP Feedback model in Chapter 3.
Start building a team charter	A team charter is a document that defines the purpose of the team, how it will work, and what the expected outcomes are. It is a 'roadmap' that the team (and potentially its sponsors) create at the beginning of the journey (or it can be done later if needed) to make sure that all involved are clear about where they're heading, and to give direction when times get tough. It is never too late to create one! It is created by the team leader together with the team members. A team charter is effective if all members of the team have an input, discussing and agreeing the contents of it and committing to live by it. And as creating a team charter is a joint process, you can create greater commitment and buy-in, and increase your chances of success for the team. We recommend you include the following in your team charter. Some of these may already be in place – if so, you need only refer to them in the workshop to ensure everyone is in agreement: ■ Purpose and clear links to organisation's vision and purpose ■ Expectations and goals ■ Roles and responsibilities ■ Skills and expertise needed (to fulfil purpose) ■ Resources needed (to fulfil purpose) ■ Operating guidelines, behaviours and how the team will work together (to fulfil purpose) ■ Signed agreement.	When building a Team Charter, keep the team focused on the task at hand. If other issues come up, 'park' them for another session, making a commitment about when these issues can be looked at.

▶

What	How	Rough timings and other considerations
Explain the purpose of the team charter	Use some of the description in the intro section above.	10–20 minutes
Draw the contents of a team charter (the bullet points above) on a flipchart	Go through each of the points in the team charter, discussing with the team and coming to conclusions and agreements.	
Purpose and clear links to organisation's vision and purpose	Here you set the scene, describing what the purpose/mission of the team is. Create the contents by discussing the following questions: ■ Why was this team formed? ■ What is our purpose/mission? ■ What opportunity, challenge or issue will/do we address? ■ How does our mission contribute to the company's overall vision?	60–90 minutes For more ideas about team purpose, review Chapter 10
Expectations and goals	Here you get specific by creating/clarifying the team's goals and what's expected of the team. Discuss questions such as these: ■ What are the specific goals for this team? ■ How will we measure our success? ■ Who are customers and stakeholders of our work? ■ What are their needs and expectations? ■ What obstacles can we expect along the way? And how can we overcome them? ■ How will we make sure we take shared responsibility and hold each other accountable for these goals?	60–90 minutes
Roles and responsibilities	Here you create clarity on what everyone in the team does. Discuss with the team: ■ How will/does each person contribute to the overall mission of the team? ■ What is each person's role and key responsibilities? ■ What are the handovers to other people inside or outside of team (to ensure an effective end-to-end delivery)?	60–90 minutes

▶

What	How	Rough timings and other considerations
Skills and expertise needed (to fulfil purpose)	Here you clarify what skills and expertise the team needs to have to get the job done. Depending on how well established the team is, consider some of these discussion subjects: ■ Refer back to your earlier discussion on strengths from the pre-work and recognise/map out strengths that can help fulfill the team's purpose ■ What skills and expertise does each person have? ■ What skills and expertise are missing? ■ What development/training they will receive/need? If relevant, this may or may not include a clarification of budget (depending on whether team members will have any insight to or responsibility for the budget).	60–90 minutes
Resources needed (to fulfil purpose)	Here you clarify what other resources are needed to get the job done. Depending on how well established the team is, consider some of these discussion subjects: ■ What resources are available to support them in their job (e.g. you, other leaders, colleagues, teams, books, internet sites etc.). ■ Ask the team if there are any needs for resources that haven't been discussed or met (manage this discussion carefully, so the team doesn't run off and start suggesting unnecessary items or 'nice to haves' that won't add value).	30–60 minutes
Operating guidelines, how the team will work together (to fulfil purpose)	Here you decide exactly how the team will work together. You explore and outline what is acceptable and not acceptable. How detailed you want to get is entirely up to you and the team. Include something on communication (how and when will communication happen from you, in what format, when will the team meet and so on). Use these questions to help the discussion: ■ How does this team need to operate in order for us enjoy working here, and achieving our goals and purpose?	60–120 minutes

What	How	Rough timings and other considerations
	▪ What do we expect of each other, day to day?	
	▪ What behaviours should we all commit to?	
	▪ What behaviours would be unacceptable?	
	▪ How will we keep ourselves and each other accountable to these guidelines?	
Signed agreement	Make notes of all agreements, including anything that has been 'parked' for later discussion.	Signing typically happens after the workshop, when the Team Charter document is completed.
Go through next steps	Summarise/share what will happen after the workshop, who will do what and when. This includes information about when to regroup and review.	20–30 minutes
Individual commitments	Finish the workshop by going around the room asking each team member to reflect on the two days, sharing what they have learned and what they will commit to going forward (e.g. support my team members, be on time, give helpful feedback, share my knowledge etc.).	20–40 minutes
Closing comments	Share your observations from the workshop; highlight the progress the team has made; praise and recognise contributions and participation. Share your commitment to the team and what you will do going forward.	10–15 minutes Your commitment and belief in what has just been created is crucial to its success. Make sure the team can see it and feel it.

What to do after the workshop

- Finalise the output from the discussions into a Team Charter Template (see http://www.leadingteamsbook.com/)
- Get all team members to sign the team charter, showing their commitment and buy-in.

- Make sure the team charter is distributed to everyone and/or placed on the wall in a central location so all can see it.
- At regular intervals:
    - spend time as a team
    - continue to build the team and get to know each other better
    - continue to give each other helpful feedback
    - review the Team Charter to ensure it is still relevant. If needed, update it – and get all to sign again.
- When new people join the team, brief them on the team charter (if possible with the help of the rest of the team so they can bring it to life with their input of the value it's brought) and get them sign it too (once they fully understand it).

For more ideas and details on how to run a team workshop, visit http://www.leadingteamsbook.com/

What did you think of this book?

We're really keen to hear from you about this book, so that we can make our publishing even better.

Please log on to the following website and leave us your feedback.

It will only take a few minutes and your thoughts are invaluable to us.

www.pearsoned.co.uk/bookfeedback

Want to know more?

Do you want to know what happened next for the various teams you've encountered in this book? Then go to http://www.leading teamsbook.com/ and find out more. Here you will also find additional resources and extra materials that can help you progress your teamwork further.

Flint, M. and Vinberg Hearn, E., *The Team Formula: A Leadership Tale of a Team Who Found Their Way*, MX Publishing, May 2013.

This is a business book told in a story format for leaders: a leadership tale. It takes place in the world of international business where, as a result of an acquisition, two companies merge creating a team, a team struggling with conflicts and dishonesty, but also showing glimpses of loyalty and hope. Stephen, the team's leader, is challenged to get them working together. In these times of change and economic downturn, it's more important than ever that he gets it right. Follow Stephen and his team on their journey through the thorny maze that all teams travel through. This is a quick, must-read for leaders and team members in any organisation. The book offers a fun, engaging and informative experience, providing opportunities for reflection as well as valuable ideas that can be implemented immediately. The story invites the reader, to look at him/herself and ask the questions: *What choices am I making? How does this apply to me and my team? What am I doing to make this team work?* The reader can easily relate to the characters and real-life situations. Everyone will recognise a part of themselves, as well as their colleagues, and leave you wanting to know what happens next: it's a page-turner! Above all, this is a book about going from intellectual understanding to a change in behaviour for everyone on the team. A little book for BIG team success.

References

Buckingham, M. and Coffman, K., *First, Break all the Rules: What the World's Great Managers do Differently* (Simon & Schuster, 1999).

Fisch, K. and McLeod, S., Video: *Shift Happens, Did you know 2014?* https://www.youtube.com/watch?v=XrJjfDUzD7M

Jeffers, S., *Feel the Fear and Do It Anyway* (Vermillion, Random House Group Ltd, 2007).

Laboratory of Neuro Imaging: Brain Trivia http://www.loni.usc.edu /about_loni/education/brain_trivia.php

Pink, D. H., *Drive: The Surprising Truth about what Motivates Us* (Canongate Books Ltd, 2010).

Reilly, R., 'Five Ways to Improve Employee Engagement', *Gallup Business Journal* January 7, 2014. http://www.gallup.com /businessjournal/166667/five-ways-improve-employee-engagement .aspx

Index